The Changing of the Garb

of the

How to Put Off the Old Man and Put On the New

Rick Carter, Jr., Ph.D.

The Changing of the Garb

of the

How to Put Off the Old Man and Put On the New

Rick Carter, Jr., Ph.D.

The Changing of the Garb

ISBN# 978-1-60208-448-3

Printed in the USA by:
FBC Publications & Printing
Fort Pierce, FL 34982
www.fbcpublications.com

Contents

Introduction

The study of how to put off the old nature and put on the new has been a consuming thing in my life for a decade. Not foremost because of others, but because I see in myself so many ways in which I should be closer to God. I long to be like Christ and there is a definite promise in the Bible that He will conform us into His image. I know that it is His work to do so but I don't want to be found fighting against Him, I want to give the Lord as much of me as He needs to accomplish His transforming work as I can.

This book is not a magic pill that can be taken, but a Biblical pattern that God wants us to follow that will give Him the access to our hearts to conform us into His glorious image. It is my prayer that as you read and apply the principles of God's Word found here your life will be transformed and you will grow closer to God in all areas of your life. Through nearly 20 years of ministry I have come to believe that the thing that matters most in our life is our intimacy with God. Sin separates that intimacy and hinders our walk with God, however most people are as close to Him as they want to be. For those who desire to be closer God has given us the opportunity.

While it is God that does the transforming work,

He commands us to be the ones to put off the old and put on the new man. This is a command for the obedient believer I challenge you not to allow the devil to convince you that victory is only available for others, you can have a closeness with God that you have never known if you apply His Word to your life as well.

CHAPTER 1

Why Do I Struggle?

I cannot begin to tell you how many times that my heart has been crushed under the weight of conviction for once again yielding to the sin that has had a stronghold on my mind and my flesh. Many times I have prayed that God would just remove the lust for those sins from my heart and set me free with the whisper of a prayer. I have often had the thought, "Since the Lord is all powerful, why doesn't He just remove sin from us? Why doesn't He just take the desire to sin away from us so that we can live holy lives without the struggle of sin?"

I have often cried as Paul did in Romans 7:24, "O wretched man that I am! who shall deliver me from the body of this death?" You see, I too with my mind serve the law of God. Within my heart I long to be holy, I desire to live a life free from the wretched sin that besets me; and yet just as Paul I find that the law of sin is still working in my members, dragging me down and reminding me every day of the destruction and death that rests within my body. The daily battle, for it cannot be described any other way, is a great weight upon the heart of anyone who has trusted Christ and desires to be pleasing to their

Saviour.

The wonderful blessing that I hold on to is that I believe that God has given us everything that pertains to life and Godliness through His Word. I believe that He has given us the answers to all of the struggles of this life and the answer for how to live a Godly life. Yet in His great wisdom, being the Creator of life, and the Designer of the heart of man, He knew that what we do not work for, we take for granted. Truly the truth is open and plain to those who seek Him and earnestly search for the answers in His Word, yet it must be that we have reached the end of ourselves before we will appropriate it. All too often we have sought to add God's answers to our own and formulate some sort of combination that is satisfactory to our flesh without causing us too much pain in change. The change that transforms however is a painful process to the flesh; and not a drop of the flesh can enter into it, or it will be contaminated and fail.

Often we have a negative and wrong view of the struggle that we face in gaining victory over sin in our lives. The book of Ephesians gives us some great insight into the Biblical process of changing from the old sinful man into the new spiritual man. We will be examining a number of different principles from Ephesians as we go on; but the first one that we must grab hold of to set the footing for the rest is found in Ephesians 5:1-2: "Be ye therefore followers of God, as dear children; And walk in love, as Christ also hath loved us, and hath given himself for us an offering and a sacrifice to God for a sweet smelling savour."

Many people are Christian in name and atheist in practice. They believe there is a God, but they are unwilling to allow Him to have full control of their lives. In effect their lives are no different than if they just denied God existed to begin with. They make all of their own decisions; they run their life by their own thinking and feelings, with little or no concern with what God's Word actually says about how to structure our lives.

The issue here in Ephesians 5 begins with the humility to recognize that God is greater than I and, as the Creator, He is the Father of all, which naturally makes me His child. He is the Father, and I am the child; I am to follow His example. A child in his innocence desires to imitate his parents. My boys, when they were little, wanted to dress up in a suit and be like daddy. My girls were always trying to wear my wife's shoes and jewelry; they wanted to be like mommy. As they began to grow they started to have a spirit of independence and wanted to be different; they developed a rebellion to what they were taught to be, and it grew to the point soon that they were in need of correction because they didn't want to do the things that they should any longer. They thought they had a better idea for running their own life. At an early stage in life, that sin nature starts to kick in and produce a natural rebellion to authority. Yet, even in the situation that they were in rebellion and receiving discipline, there was still a desire in them to be like their mom and dad. That in-born desire is in every person, unless it is killed by the foolishness and sin of the parents. That same desire is in every person to be like God. We naturally want as a child to follow Him. We naturally as a child want to be like Him, but as our flesh learns rebellion we turn away from His example and walk to the pleasing of the flesh.

After salvation we are awakened to the desire to be like our Father once again. As we learn to be like Him, God is as a good Father pointing out the wrong deeds that are present in our flesh and bringing to light the right example that He set for us through Jesus Christ. When I correct my children I say to them, "Stop doing this, and start doing that." You might say it like this, "Put off the wrong action, and put on the right action." I am asking them to turn over the right of self-determination in that area to me as their father. I am trying to teach them the actions that will lead to a quiet and peaceable life. Solomon said to his son in Proverbs 23:19, "Hear thou, my son, and be wise, and guide thine heart in the way."

Not long before the writing of this book, my oldest child hurt her foot. I expressed to her that, based upon the way that she injured it, the best course of action would be to make sure to stretch it out and use it some so that it would recover faster for her. She, however, did not believe that I knew what I was talking about and cried and protested that she was completely unable to use it in any fashion. I knew that was not the case, because I had examined it and knew that the injury was not as bad as she was expressing, and because I myself had experienced a similar injury before. My experience and examination were superior to her belief, yet she insisted that she knew better. After some time of conferring with her on the subject, she very reluctantly agreed to put the slightest amount of weight on it but let me know that she was not happy about the arrangement as she was on her way out the door to go to school. That afternoon when I got home I saw her walking normally and even running in the yard. I said to her, "I thought you couldn't use your foot." She replied, "Well, it doesn't hurt now." Had she followed her course of thought, she would have been held up lame for days; but because of yielding to my counsel, she found that before long the pain was gone. Often we protest in the same fashion with God. We think that we know better than He does how to run our lives. We listen to the lie that He just doesn't understand our particular situation, He has never experienced the problem in the same fashion that we are; and we rebel against His direction and correction. Yet we always find that when we yield our will to His, He was right, and we were wrong. His way works, and ours doesn't. God is such a loving and gracious Father that He suffers us when we are intolerable and guides us in spite of our protesting.

In Ephesians 5:2 God tells us how to follow Him - we are to walk in love. That statement is not left in ambiguity; He explains it by saying as Christ loved us. How did He love us? He gave Himself as an offering and sacrifice for us, to pay for our sin debt. This was not just a man suffering as a man; it was God suffering as a man. The message of the Bible is that God, the eternal, all powerful, immutable One, was willing to suffer and die just like us, in our place and for our salvation. He is not willing that any should perish, but He will honor their decision if they reject Him. He could have stopped it; but God has not chosen to prevent sin, He has chosen to overcome it! The same truth is applicable to the suffering that results from sin. God does not prevent suffering, but through Him we can overcome suffering.

The strange paradox of life is that peace and possessions do not give meaning to life. The lie that they do is one of the shrewdest ever told by Satan. The young people in America today have more than any generation has ever had. There is more entertainment, more possessions, and more excessive living than there has ever been. Even the poor of our culture have more than most people throughout time have ever possessed, and yet they are also some of the most miserable people ever to walk the face of planet Earth. They are depressed, they are discouraged, and they are bored. The happiest people in our day are those who endured the great depression and the world wars. They experienced terrible tragedy; they had nothing and knew what that actually meant.

I have had the great pleasure of traveling to several mission fields including Great Britton and the Philippines. In Great Britton the people, for the most part, are not particularly happy. Much like America, they have a great deal of possessions and modern convenience; yet they have very little outward joy. In the Philippines, they have very little in the way of possessions and conveniences; many live in tiny bamboo huts and don't even have running water. They live from meal to meal often and make very little money, often just enough to get by day to day. Yet, I have never been around a happier people. They have a genuine joy which is not due to having great possessions or an easy and peaceful life by American standards.

H.G. Wells, the famous historian and philosopher, said at age 61: "I have no peace. All of life is at the end of the tether." The literary genius Thoreau said, "Most men live lives of quiet desperation." Before taking his own life, Ralph Barton, one of the top cartoonists of the nations, left a note pinned to his pillow which said, "I have had few difficulties, many friends, great successes; I have gone from wife to wife, from house to house, visited great countries of the world; but I am fed up with inventing devices to fill up twenty-four hours of the day."

These men like many others have found out what Solomon found and wrote about in Ecclesiastes 2:1-11 – "I said in mine heart, Go to now, I will prove thee with mirth, therefore enjoy pleasure: and, behold, this also is vanity. I said of laughter, It is mad: and of mirth, What doeth it? I sought in mine heart to give myself unto wine, yet acquainting mine heart with wisdom; and to lay hold on folly, till I might see what was that good for the sons of men, which they should do under the heaven all the days of their life. I made me great works; I builded me houses; I planted me vineyards: I made me gardens and orchards, and I planted trees in them of all kind of fruits: I made me pools of water, to water therewith the wood that bringeth forth trees: I got me servants and maidens, and had servants born in my house; also I had great possessions of great and small cattle above all that were in Jerusalem before me: I gathered me also silver and gold, and the peculiar treasure of kings and of the provinces: I gat me men singers and women singers, and the delights of the sons of men, as musical instruments, and that of all sorts. So I was great, and increased more than all that were before me in Jerusalem: also my wisdom remained with me. And whatsoever mine eyes desired I kept not from them, I withheld not my heart from any joy; for my heart rejoiced in all my labour: and this was my portion of all my labour. Then I looked on all the works that my hands had wrought, and on the labour that I had laboured to do: and, behold, all was vanity and vexation of spirit, and there was no profit under the sun."

Meaning and joy are not the result of having; they are the result of suffering. This is the great paradox of life. God has everything; and yet the Bible says in Hebrews 12:2, " Looking unto Jesus the author and finisher of our faith; who for the joy that was set before him endured the cross, despising the shame, and is set down at the right hand of the throne of God." It was the suffering for you that brought the greatest joy to God in purchasing your salvation. Yet it is our natural concept that if we could just eliminate suffering from our lives we would be happy. We would have peace if we had everything we wanted; that is the greatest lie the devil has ever told. Peace and happiness, contentment and meaning are not tied to possessions; they are not tied to achievement; they are tied to service. Paul said in 1 Corinthians 1:20, "Where is the wise? where is the scribe? where is the disputer of this world? hath not God made foolish the wisdom of this world?"

The skeptic and agnostic would say that suffering is incompatible with the idea of an all-powerful and all-loving God, yet that is because they have not understood His own example. Suffering is the means by which God demonstrated His very love for us. And then He called it a sweet-smelling savor. It is the suffering of life that gives the rest of life its meaning and sweetness. It is the suffering that gives us the understanding of how to savor the peace. James said in James 5:11, "Behold, we count them happy which endure. Ye have heard of the patience of Job, and have seen the end of the Lord; that the Lord is very pitiful, and of tender mercy."

God, in His great wisdom, gave you the opportunity to achieve peace through the overcoming of the trial of sin in your life. If you did not know the sorrow of sin, you could not understand the bliss of victory. He gave us an example of such victory through His own sacrifice and victorious life. Jesus Christ makes His own sacrifice and victory over sin as an illustration to us of what true love is, of what true life is. Victorious life is found in the struggle of putting off sin and putting on righteousness. Joyful life is found in the suffering of the weight of removing the old man and putting on the new. It is found in having to make the conscious decision to be renewed in the spirit of our mind and resist the lust of our flesh, yielding rather to the wooing of the Spirit.

And so Paul continues in **Ephesians 5:3-13** by saying, "But fornication, and all uncleanness, or covetousness, let it not be once named among you, as becometh saints; Neither filthiness, nor foolish talking, nor jesting, which are not convenient: but rather giving of thanks. For this ye know, that no whoremonger, nor unclean person, nor covetous man, who is an idolater, hath any inheritance in the kingdom of Christ and of God. Let no man deceive you with vain words: for because of these things cometh the wrath of God upon the children of disobedience. Be not ye therefore partakers with them. For ye were sometimes darkness, but now are ye light in the Lord: walk as children of light: (For the fruit of the Spirit is in all goodness and righteousness and truth;) Proving what is acceptable unto the Lord. And have no fellowship with the unfruitful works of darkness, but rather reprove them. For it is a shame even to speak of those things which are done of them in secret. But all things that are reproved are made manifest by the light: for whatsoever doth make manifest is light."

Here are the things that you struggle against; here are the things that bring suffering into your life; here are the enemies that you must put down. It is a source of suffering to put away the lust of the flesh for fornication and uncleanness. It is a battle to remove covetousness from your thinking. Putting away the filthiness and foolish talking and jesting – by the way, that is not saying to never joke around about anything; it is saying that the jesting of filthiness, the dirty jokes, the wicked humor that this world has is to be resisted and put away from us.

Why? Because we know that no one who yields themselves to follow that form of wickedness has any part in God. They are aliens from the kingdom of Christ and of God. They have no inheritance in Him; rather they have their inheritance in the fruit of their wickedness. They are condemned by the lusts of their own foolish decision to reject God in favor of the pursuit of possessions and pleasures. In the end, they will suffer the damnation of their soul and the despair of their mind, when they at long last find that, though they achieved everything that they ever imagined and posses everything there is to posses, peace and happiness, love and meaning have eluded them, and they have nowhere left in this world's pursuits to resort.

If on the other hand you will refuse these things, and you will suffer their loss, choosing rather the path of God, you will follow after the example of Christ, you will do as Paul shows us here in Ephesians 5:14-21, "Wherefore he saith, Awake thou that sleepest, and arise from the dead, and Christ shall give thee light. See then that ye walk circumspectly, not as fools, but as wise, Redeeming the time, because the days are evil. Wherefore be ye not unwise, but understanding what the will of the Lord is. And be not drunk with wine, wherein is excess; but be filled with the Spirit; Speaking to yourselves in psalms and hymns and spiritual songs, singing and making melody in your heart to the Lord; Giving thanks always for all things unto God and the Father in the name of our Lord Jesus Christ; Submitting yourselves one to another in the fear of God."

— Right now could you determine that the path of indulgence this world has offered you has not provided what it promised, and God's way, though it seems contrary to your thinking, does work. You must determine to change course in His direction. There is a great opportunity for you to experience the joy of victory as you put off that old man and his sinful deeds and suffer the pain of the struggle to put on the new man daily, breaking the grip that the old man has had on your soul by crucifying the flesh, as Paul put it in Galatians 2:20, "I am crucified with Christ: nevertheless I live; yet not I, but Christ liveth in me: and the life which I now live in the flesh I live by the faith of the Son of God, who loved me, and gave himself for me."

The offering that we give to God of sacrificing the old sinful nature and putting on the new and glorified nature is a sweet smelling savor to God, and the source of joy and victory for us. There is a great blessing in knowing the power of His resurrection experienced in our victory over sin. Paul summarizes it far better than I could when he says in Philippians 3:7-14, "But what things were gain to me, those I counted loss for Christ. Yea doubtless, and I count all things but loss for the excellency of the knowledge of Christ Jesus my Lord: for whom I have suffered the loss of all things, and do count them but dung, that I may win Christ, And be found in him, not having mine own righteousness, which is of the law, but that which is through the faith of Christ, the righteousness which is of God by faith: That I may know him, and the power of his resurrection, and the fellowship of his sufferings, being made conformable unto his death; If by any means I might attain unto the resurrection of the dead. Not as though I had already attained, either were already perfect: but I follow after, if that I may apprehend that for which also I am apprehended of Christ Jesus. Brethren, I count not myself to have apprehended: but this one thing I do, forgetting those things which are behind, and reaching forth unto those things which are before, I press toward the mark for the prize of the high calling of God in Christ Jesus."

CHAPTER 2

Breaking the Cycle

If we are indeed to gain the victory over the old nature, we must break the cycle of the flesh that we are seemingly trapped in. To do that, we must understand the nature of our actions and what is behind them. The conflict with the old nature centers on specific sins for each of us. The sins vary from person to person, each of us being drawn after differing lusts. James says in James 1:14, "But every man is tempted, when he is drawn away of his own lust, and enticed." We each have a propensity toward a different sin, we each lust in what we think to be our own way; and yet our lusts are surprisingly similar. The devil is very sly at isolating us from recognizing that our sin is the same as others. A person who is given to the appetite for alcohol, for instance, believes the lie that he is the only one who has had his specific problems and therefore no one else could understand him or help him. A similar lie is told for every sin that mankind engages in.

These habitual sins form a bondage to the soul, they form a prison to the mind that constructs walls that seem stronger than steel. A steel bar may seem to be impenetrable; however, it is easier to believe that someone could come and cut that steel away than it is to believe that someone could remove the bars of lies that hold our hearts and minds captive. The basis of the problem is that we often can see the actions that we are taking are wrong, but struggle in the changing of the actions. For that reason we butt continually up against the confession cycle. This is that cycle that believers go through where they recognize the sinful actions and are sorry for doing them, ask God to forgive them, ask God to remove the desire for those things away from them, and seek earnestly to change their actions, all the while failing and falling back into the same trap again and again. In most situations they believe that they have repented and it just doesn't work for them. As a young pastor, I had an older couple join my church. One Sunday night I preached on the importance of using the altar; and, following the service, the husband asked if he could talk to me. He was a very gracious man and kind, but he wanted me to know that years earlier when he was young he had tried using the altar many times. He said, "Preacher, I had some things in my life that I knew shouldn't be there, so I went to the altar time after time and wept and prayed and asked God to remove them. But finally I realized that I was just going to have to live with them; so I have never been back to the altar since, and I don't plan on ever going again."

His experience, I believe, is very common; and it is also very sad. The confession cycle begins with an individual seeing that there is some action in his life that is sinful, and he is convicted in his soul that he should remove or change it. The problem is that he is stuck in the habitual process of it; and he does not understand that getting freedom over a habitual sin requires more than just seeing an action that is a problem, but seeing the root of the problem, which is what produces the action.

It isn't as simple as "just don't do that"; the complication of addiction and habit are strong barriers to moving from one action to another. The old idea of "just stop it" just doesn't work. The issue runs deeper than just our actions. Every action is supported by pillars of belief, and our beliefs are formed and supported by our thinking. Proverbs 23:7 says, "For as he thinketh in his heart, so is he: Eat and drink, saith he to thee; but his heart is not with thee." The thoughts of the heart form the pillars of belief upon which your actions will be based. I don't know of anyone who would look at his wrong actions and say, "The reason that I do this is because I have knowingly believed a series of complicated lies and based my life upon them." Yet that is exactly what our wrong actions are based upon. Our sinful actions and habits that we struggle against, that war against the spiritual man are all because we have allowed the foundation of lies to gird together false beliefs. Not willingly or knowingly – if you knew it was a lie you would have rejected it, you would even now reject it – but within your thinking and mine there rest the seeds of lies that we have unwittingly accepted. The reason that we cannot seem to rid ourselves of the sinful actions of the flesh is because that old sin nature has so deceived our thinking that we do not recognize the truth.

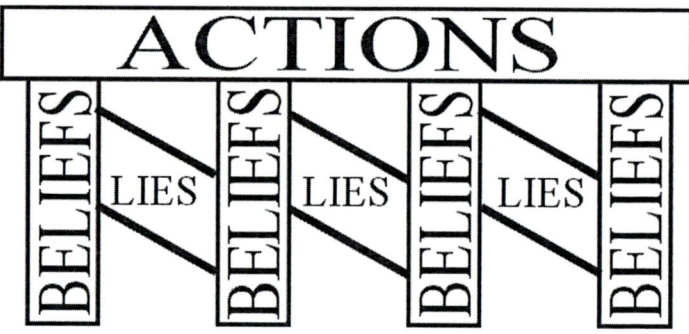

It is not enough to just change your actions; the root problem is a thinking problem to begin with. Listen to what Paul said in Romans 12:1-3: "I beseech you therefore, brethren, by the mercies of God, that ye present your bodies a living sacrifice, holy, acceptable unto God, which is your reasonable service. And be not conformed to this world: but be ye transformed by the renewing of your mind, that ye may prove what is that good, and acceptable, and perfect, will of God. For I say, through the grace given unto me, to every man that is among you, not to think of himself more highly than he ought to think; but to think soberly, according as God hath dealt to every man the measure of faith."

Notice that when Paul beseeches us to present our bodies as a living sacrifice to God he doesn't say, "And change all your actions"; rather he says, "Renew your mind." He follows that up with not to think of yourself more highly than you ought to think, but to think soberly. Immediately following the admonition to present our bodies to God, we are challenged to renew the mind and our thinking; that is because it is the thinking that ultimately determines the actions of the body. Your body is a responder to your mind; it is yielded to the process of your thoughts. Therefore there is no mystery that when you have believed wrong facts, your thoughts are affected after those things and form errant beliefs, which in turn result in wrong actions. It doesn't matter how much you want to change your actions. Until you get to the root lie that caused the sinful thinking problem, it will be a temporary change at best; and the confession cycle will continue until we get frustrated and give up.

Paul deals with the issue of our thoughts over and over again in the New Testament. 2 Corinthians 10:3-6 tells us, "For though we walk in the flesh, we do not war after the flesh: (For the weapons of our warfare are not carnal, but mighty through God to the pulling down of strong holds;) Casting down imaginations, and every high thing that exalteth itself against the knowledge of God, and bringing into captivity every thought to the obedience of Christ; And having in a readiness to revenge all disobedience, when your obedience is fulfilled." The issue that we always want to deal with is the flesh; but Paul points out here that the battle is not really a battle of the flesh, it is a battle for control of the mind. Whoever controls your thinking controls your actions. If you want to remove the strong hold that a particular sin has over your flesh, you must attack it at the thought level. *No, Take up your cross*

We use the word *repentance* to express the changing of the thoughts to conform to the Word of God. The Webster's 1828 dictionary says that repentance is a change of mind, or a conversion from sin to God. Feeling bad about doing something is not the same as changing your mind about doing it. The difference is that true repentance deals with the underlying issues of the mind; it attacks the problem at its source and identifies the lies and replaces them with truth. Until you replace the lies with truth, you will never effectively change your beliefs, and thus your actions will ultimately remain the same. The old man spoken of in Colossians is more than just what you do; read again in Colossians 3:9, "Lie not one to another, seeing that ye have put off the old man with his deeds." The deeds of the old man are not his nature; they are the result of his nature; they are the result of his old lustful thinking. If we are to put off the deeds of the old man we must first put off the old man. His deeds follow him.

 I want you to know that victory is attainable for you over the deeds of the old man. In His Word, God has given us all things that pertain to life and Godliness. The devil is a master at taking away hope that you can get victory over the sins that you struggle with. In Hebrews 12:1 it says, "Wherefore seeing we also are compassed about with so great a cloud of witnesses, let us lay aside every weight, and the sin which doth so easily beset us, and let us run with patience the race that is set before us." This verse is a source of great strength to the believer that accepts the promise of the Scripture, that God would not tell us to do something that is not possible. Here He tells us to lay aside the sin that so easily besets us; that means it is possible to lay it aside. Though you may have tried before, though you may have failed before this, it doesn't mean that it is impossible to do. If you think that it is, that is because you have allowed the devil to plant the seed of that lie in your thinking. You must remember 1 John 4:4: "Ye are of God, little children, and have overcome them: because greater is he that is in you, than he that is in the world."

Philippians 4:13 tells us, "I can do all things through Christ which strengtheneth me." The first thing that you must confirm before you can have the strength of Christ to overcome the deeds of the old man is that Christ is indeed in you. The issue of salvation is not something that can be overlooked in this issue of victory over the sinful deeds of the flesh. A man who is not saved is trying to fight the flesh with the flesh, which will never work. Before we go on in our study of putting off the old man, let us first examine ourselves in this matter for a moment.

It is clear in the Scriptures that salvation is not the result of a process of actions. A man cannot be good enough, religious enough, or righteous enough in his own flesh to attain salvation. It is not the result of repeating a prayer, being baptized, or some mystical and magical experience. So many are trusting in some experience that they have had, rather than trusting in Christ Jesus. Let me say that nowhere in the Bible is assurance of salvation based upon what you remember or how you feel. I have spoken to many people who told me, "I doubt my salvation." When asked why, they say things like, "I just don't feel saved." The struggle comes when they say, "But I remember praying." Hold on a minute – if that is what you are basing your salvation on, you are going to be in a continual crisis. The devil can give you an experience and a feeling; that is not what God is speaking of when He says that we must be born again. Biblical assurance of salvation is found in Romans 8:16, "The Spirit itself beareth witness with our spirit, that we are the children of God."

The assurance of salvation is not a feeling or a memory; it is a knowing. It is the result of the Spirit of God being in you and speaking to your spirit. If your assurance is based upon anything else, you are in trouble. You might remember or feel yourself right into hell! I have sat with people who were just as lost as a goose, they were living in all sort of wickedness without the slightest bit of conviction or judgment, they spurned the thought that God cared how they lived; and yet they were just as adamant that they were saved as anyone I have ever met. I would ask them, "Is there any judgment in your life for your sin; is there any indication that you have that God is displeased with what you are doing?" Of course there is not from what they can see. God has an answer for that in Hebrews 12:5-8, "And ye have forgotten the exhortation which speaketh unto you as unto children, My son, despise not thou the chastening of the Lord, nor faint when thou art rebuked of him: For whom the Lord loveth he chasteneth, and scourgeth every son whom he receiveth. If ye endure chastening, God dealeth with you as with sons; for what son is he whom the father chasteneth not? But if ye be without chastisement, whereof all are partakers, then are ye bastards, and not sons."

The way to know if you are saved is not to see if you remember some event, nor is it to have some feeling; it is to bow your head and pray to God, asking Him to bear witness with you as to your salvation or lack of it. I have dealt with many who were in doubt about their salvation; as long as you are in doubt you can do nothing. I have bowed in prayer with many and prayed for the Lord to take away the confusion. As they prayed and asked the Lord to confirm or deny their salvation, I have had both take place. Some have stopped mid-prayer and said, "Pastor, He is there; I know it. I don't know why I ever doubted it." Not because of a feeling, but because His Spirit bore witness with theirs. I have also had people stop and say, "Pastor, I am just as lost as can be. If I died right now, I would go to hell; I have no doubt." Then they were able to get saved. Let me remind you that God is not the author of confusion. If there is confusion, it is the work of the devil.

Salvation is as simple as this – you must agree with God about your sin and cast yourself upon Him for mercy through the death, burial, and resurrection of Jesus Christ according to the Scriptures.

You don't deserve forgiveness, you cannot earn it; but God longs to give it to you. He wants you to know His love that was given on the cross of Calvary through His only begotten Son. If you have never received Christ to be your Saviour, you can even now. Simply obey the Bible when it says in Romans 10:9-10, "That if thou shalt confess with thy mouth the Lord Jesus, and shalt believe in thine heart that God hath raised him from the dead, thou shalt be saved. For with the heart man believeth unto righteousness; and with the mouth confession is made unto salvation." If you are in confusion about your salvation, you can have clarity even now. Bow your head and ask God to confirm by His Spirit within you whether you are saved or not. Let Him confirm your condition; and if you are lost, receive Him immediately.

Once you have settled this issue of salvation, you can begin to take the steps that the Bible outlines about how to truly put off the old man and his deeds. You can have the victory in Jesus that you have longed for, if you will obey His Word as His child.

CHAPTER 3

Who is God?

There is no way to fully explain or completely exhaust the question "Who is God?" Surely not in a single chapter – this is not an attempt to do that, but simply to give an understanding as to the image of God that is presented in the Bible. The purpose of this is to help us understand the image that we were created in. As we consider God's image, we can better see our own and learn about the way in which we were intended to function. If you have an item that isn't working the way it is supposed to, comparing it to what is working properly can help to identify some of the defects that need to be corrected. Asking the question "Who is God?" is an attempt to do that.

The Bible teaches us in many places that God is a trinity. **1 John 5:7** says, "For there are three that bear record in heaven, the Father, the Word, and the Holy Ghost: and these three are one." In the beginning of creation we see the trinity present. The Bible says in **John 1:1-3**, "In the beginning was the Word, and the Word was with God, and the Word was God. The same was in the beginning with God. All things were made by him; and without him was not any thing made that was made." In **Genesis 1:1-2** it says, "In the beginning God created the heaven and the earth. And the earth was without form, and void; and darkness was upon the face of the deep. And the Spirit of God moved upon the face of the waters." Here you see the Father in the intellect and wisdom, the Son in the word, and the Spirit moving in the creative process.

God the Father is the soul of God, the center of His being. The soul is made up of three parts. The soul is made first of the intellect, that is, how God thinks. **Psalm 139:17** says, "How precious also are thy thoughts unto me, O God! how great is the sum of them!" All the thoughts of God proceed from the Father. When Jesus spoke to the Father, He was consulting with the Father as to what His thoughts and will were on the issues that He in the flesh was facing. The thoughts of God are far superior to our feeble thinking. As a matter of fact, God said in Isaiah 55:9, "For as the heavens are higher than the earth, so are my ways higher than your ways, and my thoughts than your thoughts." The thoughts of God are so superior to our own that we couldn't possibly understand them all. As a matter of fact, the Bible is a revelation of the thoughts of God that we could understand; but we don't really even understand all of it completely. God is omniscient – that means all-knowing. He is also righteous, which means that He has no sin at all. All the thoughts of God are pure and right, which is something that we cannot say about our own. In our sinful condition, the thoughts of God contained in the Bible don't make sense; but when we admit that He is right and we are wrong, when we turn to Him, His thoughts begin to make sense though we will still never know or understand them all.

The soul is not only the thinking but also made up of the emotions – that is, how God feels. **Psalm 7:11** says, "God judgeth the righteous, and God is angry with the wicked every day." **John 15:9** says, "As the Father hath loved me, so have I loved you: continue ye in my love." These and many other verses show that the Father experiences emotion just as we do; as a matter of fact, our emotions are from Him. The difference is that He has no sin, so He does not respond to emotion in a sinful manner. Emotions are not right or wrong; they are able to be used in a right or wrong way though. God is angry, but God never sins; thus God's anger is righteous, and He uses it to accomplish what is right. God says to us in Ephesians 4:26, "Be ye angry, and sin not: let not the sun go down upon your wrath." If you responded to anger like God does, you would not respond in sin. The same is true for all emotion. The problem is that we often allow our emotion to rule our lives, or we allow our sinful thinking to motivate us through our emotions, and thus we commit sin. God the Father demonstrates to us the proper use of emotions in the Scriptures.

The third and final part of the soul is formed from the first two; it is the volition or will. How God thinks and how He feels determine what He decides to do. Jesus said in **John 5:30**, "I can of mine own self do nothing: as I hear, I judge: and my judgment is just; because I seek not mine own will, but the will of the Father which hath sent me." The will of God is a topic of much discussion in the Bible; it is His will which we are each to follow, just as Jesus demonstrated for us. The will of God is revealed in His Word. It says in Romans 12:2, "And be not conformed to this world: but be ye transformed by the renewing of your mind, that ye may prove what is that good, and acceptable, and perfect, will of God." We will talk later in this book about how to be transformed by the renewing of your mind, but I want you to know that God the Father has a specific will for your life that He wants you to know.

Part of the Father's will was accomplished when He sent the Son into this world to be our Saviour, because of His great love for us. **John 3:16** tells us, "For God so loved the world, that he gave his only begotten Son, that whosoever believeth in him should not perish, but have everlasting life." Jesus is the body of God. He is the physical example of God to us, so that we could see how God would respond to this world if He were here in our place. Jesus said in **John 14:6-11**, "Jesus saith unto him, I am the way, the truth, and the life: no man cometh unto the Father, but by me. If ye had known me, ye should have known my Father also: and from henceforth ye know him, and have seen him. Philip saith unto him, Lord, shew us the Father, and it sufficeth us. Jesus saith unto him, Have I been so long time with you, and yet hast thou not known me, Philip? he that hath seen me hath seen the Father; and how sayest thou then, Shew us the Father? Believest thou not that I am in the Father, and the Father in me? the words that I speak unto you I speak not of myself: but the Father that dwelleth in me, he doeth the works. Believe me that I am in the Father, and the Father in me: or else believe me for the very works' sake." When you read the Gospels, you are seeing the very way that God would respond to all of the circumstances of life through the example of Jesus.

Jesus was not only our example of how God would respond to life, but He was also the example of how we should respond as well. **John 8:29** says, "And he that sent me is with me: the Father hath not left me alone; for I do always those things that please him." When you look at the life of Jesus, you are seeing a pattern of how to please God the Father. The Christian life is Christ; it is living as He lived, doing what He did, and loving as He loved. Living the Christian life is not about a list of do's and don'ts; it is about emulating Him and what He would do based upon the example that we see in His Word. Paul said it like this in **Romans 13:14**: "But put ye on the Lord Jesus Christ, and make not provision for the flesh, to fulfil the lusts thereof." To live the Christian life, we must learn to put on the Lord Jesus Christ in the place of our fleshly desires and old nature. The only way to do this is to know Him intimately, and the only way to do that is to study His Word and spend time with Him in prayer. That is what this book is all about, teaching you how to know Him.

After Jesus left this earth, He did not want you to have to be alone as a believer; so He sent the Holy Spirit to indwell all believers. The Holy Spirit is called by several names in the Bible including the Holy Ghost, the Spirit, and the Comforter. It says in **John 16:7**, "Nevertheless I tell you the truth; It is expedient for you that I go away: for if I go not away, the Comforter will not come unto you; but if I depart, I will send him unto you." The sense of this verse is not that Jesus was going to send some other kind of comforter to them, but rather another of the same kind. The Holy Spirit is the Spirit of God; He is the one that speaks to you and ministers to your spirit now, just as Jesus spoke, ministered, and comforted the disciples when He was with them. As a matter of fact Jesus said in John 14:23, "Jesus answered and said unto him, If a man love me, he will keep my words: and my Father will love him, and we will come unto him, and make our abode with him." The Comforter is the Holy Spirit of God, which is how God chose to manifest Himself to us now.

If Jesus would have stayed on this earth He would have been limited by His human body. He could have only ministered to a few at a time; though He taught multitudes, He would have been limited in how many people He could minister to at any one point in time. However, as the Holy Spirit, He is now without limitation. He can minister to me in my need at my home and you to your need at your home, and it doesn't matter how far apart we are. He is not limited to speak about only one topic at a time; He can speak to me about what troubles me on one topic and to you about a completely different topic.

Jesus explained a little bit of what work the Holy Spirit would do in **John 16:8-11**, "And when he is come, he will reprove the world of sin, and of righteousness, and of judgment: Of sin, because they believe not on me; Of righteousness, because I go to my Father, and ye see me no more; Of judgment, because the prince of this world is judged."

One of the first jobs that the Holy Spirit does is

to draw men to repentance. He does this in three ways according to this passage of scripture. First, He reproves of sin, meaning that He shows us that it is wrong. Paul tells us in **Romans 2:15**, "Which shew the work of the law written in their hearts, their conscience also bearing witness, and their thoughts the mean while accusing or else excusing one another." The heart of every man has God's law written on it, so that they are without excuse before God for their sin. Not only that, but when we are saved the Holy Spirit continues to write on our heart according to **2 Corinthians 3:3** – "Forasmuch as ye are manifestly declared to be the epistle of Christ ministered by us, written not with ink, but with the Spirit of the living God; not in tables of stone, but in fleshy tables of the heart." In this way the Holy Spirit writes the righteousness of Christ upon us. It is not enough to see that one thing is wrong; God wants us to know what is right as well. This is the righteousness that Jesus was speaking of when He spoke in John 16. Finally, He said that the Holy Spirit would teach us of judgment. The reason that God does not rid the world of sin right now is so that we will see the consequences of it before our eyes and know that God judges sin. The result of sin is devastating; and by seeing it every day, we can know that God is serious about judgment and one day will judge all those who have rejected the gift of eternal life through Jesus Christ, because they have chosen to stay in their sin. They will be judged with the devil and have the same fate that he is due.

The Holy Spirit is not trying to draw us to Himself; the Spirit isn't interested in getting attention or glory for Himself even though He is God. The Holy Spirit wants the attention to go to Jesus. Jesus said in **John 15:26**, "But when the Comforter is come, whom I will send unto you from the Father, even the Spirit of truth, which proceedeth from the Father, he shall testify of me." The Holy Spirit never seeks to draw attention to Himself; He always points people to Christ. Christ in turn points us to the Father, as everything He did was to bring us to the Father. He said in **John 14:6**, "Jesus saith unto him, I am the way, the truth, and the life: no man cometh unto the Father, but by me." He also taught us to pray to the Father by saying in **Matthew 6:9**, "After this manner therefore pray ye: Our Father which art in heaven, Hallowed be thy name."

The example of the Godhead is so that each one points to the work of the other. That is the perfect example that God seeks for us to learn as well, that we would not point to what we do, but to what He does. The Christian life is not about you; it is about Him. If you can understand that simple truth, it will make your life with Him a great joy. If you are self-focused and seek to make what you do or don't do in your Christian life about you, then you will find it to be a hard life, because God never intended it to be lived like that.

This is just a small picture into who God is, but it will suffice to give us the understanding that we are needing in this study. You will spend the rest of your life learning about Him and getting to know Him, as He longs for you to have an intimate personal relationship with Him. That relationship develops and deepens each day as you read His Word and learn more and more about who He is.

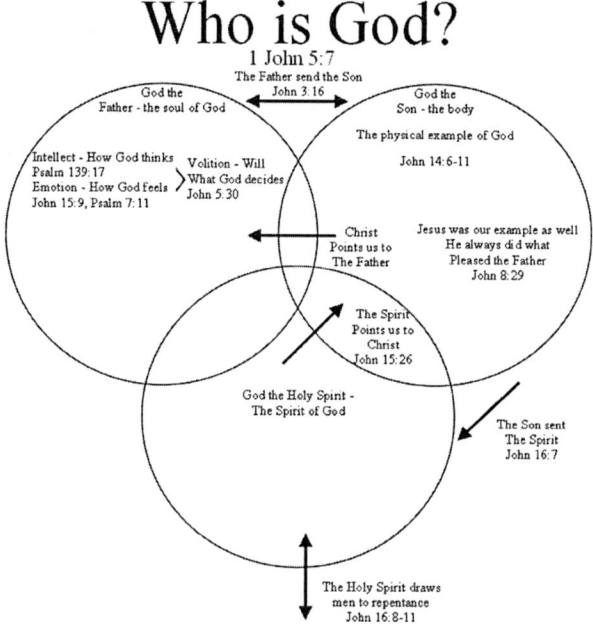

Who is God?

1 John 5:7
The Father send the Son
John 3:16

God the
Father - the soul of God

Intellect - How God thinks
Psalm 139:17
Emotion - How God feels
John 15:9, Psalm 7:11

Volition - Will
What God decides
John 5:30

God the
Son - the body

The physical example of God
John 14:6-11

Christ
Points us to
The Father

Jesus was our example as well
He always did what
Pleased the Father
John 8:29

The Spirit
Points us to
Christ
John 15:26

God the Holy Spirit -
The Spirit of God

The Son sent
The Spirit
John 16:7

The Holy Spirit draws
men to repentance
John 16:8-11

Man

CHAPTER 4

Who is Man?

Genesis 1:26-27 says, "And God said, Let us make man in our image, after our likeness: and let them have dominion over the fish of the sea, and over the fowl of the air, and over the cattle, and over all the earth, and over every creeping thing that creepeth upon the earth. So God created man in his own image, in the image of God created he him; male and female created he them."

We were created in the image of God; that is why it is important that you understand first what God's image is as we studied last week. You cannot understand the creature until you know the Creator. Just as God has three parts, He created us as a triune being as well. We also have a soul, a body, and a spirit. You are more than just your physical body, and you are more than just your mind. You were created to be in the very image of God.

The soul is your self conscience – it is how you know who you are. Just as in God the Father, the soul is made up first of your intellect, how you think as it says in **Romans 2:15**, "Which shew the work of the law written in their hearts, their conscience also bearing witness, and their thoughts the mean while accusing or else excusing one another." The soul is secondly made of your emotions, how you feel. Your emotions and intellect are given to you from God; but God does not want you to use them to run your life, rather He wants you to submit them to Him and His Word. The intellect and emotions together form your volition or will. That is how you decide what to do about what you think and how you feel. In the Bible, the terms heart, soul, and mind are used interchangeably to speak about these three areas. It says in **Proverbs 23:7**, "For as he thinketh in his heart, so is he: Eat and drink, saith he to thee; but his heart is not with thee." Do not confuse the soul with the body. The brain is a physical organ that God uses to store our memories and knowledge, but the brain is not your soul. Your brain will die with your body; but your soul, who you are, what you think, and how you feel will live on in eternity somewhere.

The soul needs to be saved from the debt of sin. Your soul was created by God to be eternal. When the Bible speaks of salvation, it is speaking of the forgiveness of the soul from sin. That is accomplished first by acknowledging that you are a sinner. **Romans 3:23** says, "For all have sinned, and come short of the glory of God." Secondly, you must realize that your sin has with it the consequence of eternal death. **Romans 6:23a** says, "For the wages of sin is death." **Revelation 20:11** tells us, "And I saw a great white throne, and him that sat on it, from whose face the earth and the heaven fled away; and there was found no place for them. And I saw the dead, small and great, stand before God; and the books were opened: and another book was opened, which is the book of life: and the dead were judged out of those things which were written in the books, according to their works. And the sea gave up the dead which were in it; and death and hell delivered up the dead which were in them: and they were judged every man according to their works. And death and hell were cast into the lake of fire. This is the second death. And whosoever was not found written in the book of life was cast into the lake of fire." The third thing that you must know is that Jesus was crucified, buried, and rose again according to the Scriptures to pay the debt of sin that you owed. **Romans 6:23b** says, "But the gift of God is eternal life through Jesus Christ our Lord." To receive Christ as the payment for your sin, you must repent of your sin and confess your faith in Him to be your Saviour. **Romans 10:9-13** says, "That if thou shalt confess with thy mouth the Lord Jesus, and shalt believe in thine heart that God hath raised him from the dead, thou shalt be saved. For with the heart man believeth unto righteousness; and with the mouth confession is made unto salvation.

For the scripture saith, Whosoever believeth on him shall not be ashamed. For there is no difference between the Jew and the Greek: for the same Lord over all is rich unto all that call upon him. For whosoever shall call upon the name of the Lord shall be saved." Salvation is not a process of your works or something that you earn. It is a gift that was given to you by the sacrifice of Jesus Christ on the cross; but, like every gift, before it is yours, it must be received by you.

The body is your physical conscience – it is how you relate to the world around you. The soul must be saved, but the body never will be. One day it will be changed, however, when Christ returns for those who are saved. **1 Corinthians 15:49-54** tells us, "And as we have borne the image of the earthy, we shall also bear the image of the heavenly. Now this I say, brethren, that flesh and blood cannot inherit the kingdom of God; neither doth corruption inherit incorruption. Behold, I shew you a mystery; We shall not all sleep, but we shall all be changed, In a moment, in the twinkling of an eye, at the last trump: for the trumpet shall sound, and the dead shall be raised incorruptible, and we shall be changed. For this corruptible must put on incorruption, and this mortal must put on immortality. So when this corruptible shall have put on incorruption, and this mortal shall have put on immortality, then shall be brought to pass the saying that is written, Death is swallowed up in victory."

Sin is committed by both the body and the soul. **Isaiah 53:5** teaches us, "But he was wounded for our transgressions, he was bruised for our iniquities: the chastisement of our peace was upon him; and with his stripes we are healed." Wounds were the physical results of transgressions in Jesus. Transgressions are the physical sins that we commit; they are outside the body. Bruises are the inward consequence of our iniquities. Iniquities are the inward sins of the soul; they are the sins of the heart and the mind. Not every wrong thought is a sin; however, God says in Hebrews 4:12 that His Word can divide between the point that a thought becomes an intent and thus an iniquity – "For the word of God is quick, and powerful, and sharper than any twoedged sword, piercing even to the dividing asunder of soul and spirit, and of the joints and marrow, and is a discerner of the thoughts and intents of the heart."

The third and final part that God created you with is the spirit. Every man is born with a spiritual conscience. This is how you can have fellowship with other spirits of both men and devils. **Ephesians 2:2** shows us that, before we were saved, we were in fellowship with other spirits when it says, "Wherein in time past ye walked according to the course of this world, according to the prince of the power of the air, the spirit that now worketh in the children of disobedience." There is a spirit that works in all men, even lost men. **1 Timothy 4:1** says, "Now the Spirit speaketh expressly, that in the latter times some shall depart from the faith, giving heed to seducing spirits, and doctrines of devils." Often, you will hear someone speak of a close friend in this manner, saying that they are a kindred spirit. In saying that, they are right; your spirit can have fellowship with the spirit of other men. That is why you are drawn to some people and you are repulsed by others. This is why we have axioms such as "birds of a feather flock together." People have a tendency to naturally drift toward people of the same type of spirit, without ever having to speak to one another. You are drawn to others by the communion of your spirit. Likewise a lost man can and often will have fellowship with the unclean spirits of devils, though often unknowingly. Often, when a person accepts Christ, they say that they feel as though a great weight has been lifted off of them. This may be the unclean spirits that have been oppressing them leaving; and, for the first time in a long while, they are free from a burden that they didn't even know they had.

While the spirit of a lost man can fellowship with that of other men and of devils, it cannot fellowship with God. The Bible explains this in **Ephesians 2:1**, "And you hath he quickened, who were dead in trespasses and sins." We are spiritually dead to God so that there is no fellowship between us. This happened when Adam and Eve sinned in the Garden. They had been warned according to **Genesis 2:17**, "But of the tree of the knowledge of good and evil, thou shalt not eat of it: for in the day that thou eatest thereof thou shalt surely die." They did not drop down physically, and they did not go emotionally dead; but spiritually they died and were unable to fellowship with God any longer because of their sin. This is why God expelled them from the garden. This is why the Holy Spirit is calling to men to be saved; and when a person accepts the gift of Jesus Christ as the payment for their sins, they are born again in the spirit toward God. **John 3:3-7**, "Jesus answered and said unto him, Verily, verily, I say unto thee, Except a man be born again, he cannot see the kingdom of God. Nicodemus saith unto him, How can a man be born when he is old? can he enter the second time into his mother's womb, and be born? Jesus answered, Verily, verily, I say unto thee, Except a man be born of water and of the Spirit, he cannot enter into the kingdom of God. That which is born of the flesh is flesh; and that which is born of the Spirit is spirit. Marvel not that I said unto thee, Ye must be born again."

1 Thessalonians 5:23 tells us, "And the very God of peace sanctify you wholly; and I pray God your whole spirit and soul and body be preserved blameless unto the coming of our Lord Jesus Christ." After a person is born again, God sanctifies them beginning in the spirit, then the soul, and then the body. After salvation, the spirit that has been born again is alive toward God; and it is God's desire to have fellowship with you through the Spirit. **Romans 8:16** says, "The Spirit itself beareth witness with our spirit, that we are the children of God." This fellowship with the Spirit of God with our spirit is where assurance comes from. Assurance of salvation is not a memory or an emotion; it is a knowing in the spirit of man that is given by the fellowship of the Holy Spirit of God.

God does not expect a saved person to never sin again. He knows that you will still sin, because your body is not yet changed; and you must learn to put off the old man. He made provision for you when you sin in **1 John 1:9** when He said, "If we confess our sins, he is faithful and just to forgive us our sins, and to cleanse us from all unrighteousness." You do not need to be re-saved; salvation is a one-time thing – you just need to acknowledge to Him that you have sinned and know that it was wrong. His blood has already covered the penalty of those sins; but God wants us to keep a clean heart before Him, so that we will not allow our fellowship to slip away. There are two things that can cause your fellowship to slip with God. The first is to allow unconfessed sin to remain in your life. When you sin, you will not want to be around God. Though all of your sins are forgiven, this is not a license to sin all you want. As a matter of fact, Paul said in **Romans 6:1-2**, "What shall we say then? Shall we continue in sin, that grace may abound? God forbid. How shall we, that are dead to sin, live any longer therein?"

There are two things that will cause you to have doubts about your salvation. The first is allowing sin to remain unconfessed in your life; the second is to fail to walk with God. The lack of fellowship with God in prayer, Bible study, and church attendance will cause you to drift away from a close union with Him; and you will soon question His presence, not because He is not there, but because you have not been speaking to Him or listening to Him. When you find yourself in a place that you have doubts about your salvation, you need to come before Him and confess any sin that you know of and get back in fellowship with Him through His Word and prayer. It is not enough to just go to church; even though you go, you need a daily time of fellowship with God to grow in a proper way. In times of doubt, after confessing and drawing close to God, ask the Holy Spirit of God to bear witness with your spirit about His presence. He is a real and abiding presence within each believer.

Who is man?
Genesis 1:26-27

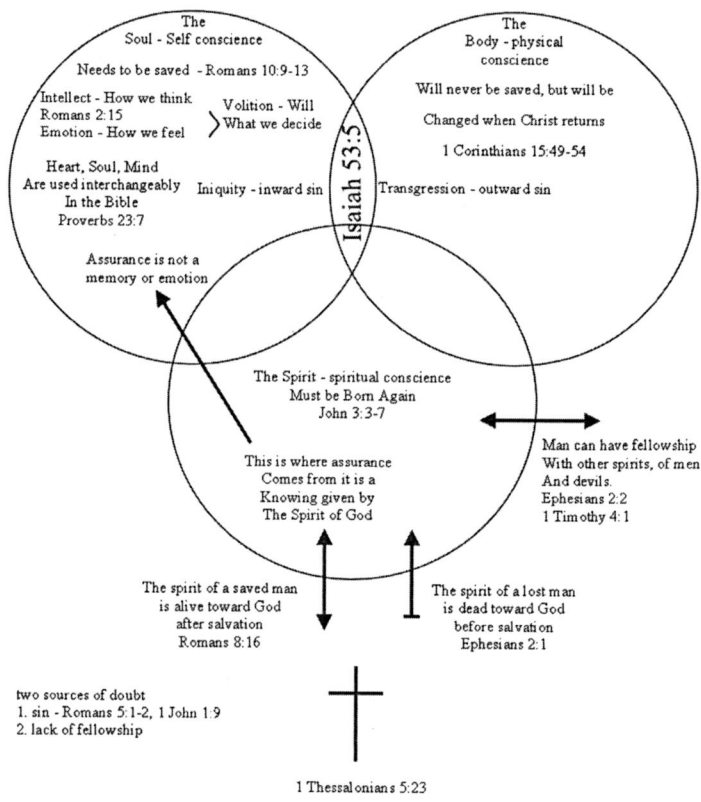

The
Soul - Self conscience

Needs to be saved - Romans 10:9-13

Intellect - How we think
Romans 2:15
Emotion - How we feel
Volition - Will
What we decide

Heart, Soul, Mind
Are used interchangeably
In the Bible
Proverbs 23:7
Iniquity - inward sin

Isaiah 53:5

Assurance is not a
memory or emotion

The
Body - physical
conscience

Will never be saved, but will be

Changed when Christ returns

1 Corinthians 15:49-54

Transgression - outward sin

The Spirit - spiritual conscience
Must be Born Again
John 3:3-7

This is where assurance
Comes from it is a
Knowing given by
The Spirit of God

Man can have fellowship
With other spirits, of men
And devils.
Ephesians 2:2
1 Timothy 4:1

The spirit of a saved man
is alive toward God
after salvation
Romans 8:16

The spirit of a lost man
is dead toward God
before salvation
Ephesians 2:1

two sources of doubt
1. sin - Romans 5:1-2, 1 John 1:9
2. lack of fellowship

1 Thessalonians 5:23

CHAPTER 5

Getting an Understanding of Our Old Man

Ephesians 4:17-19 says, "This I say therefore, and testify in the Lord, that ye henceforth walk not as other Gentiles walk, in the vanity of their mind, Having the understanding darkened, being alienated from the life of God through the ignorance that is in them, because of the blindness of their heart: Who being past feeling have given themselves over unto lasciviousness, to work all uncleanness with greediness."

Paul is getting ready in this chapter to teach us how to put off the old man and put on the new man; and in preparation for that he tells us that we are to "walk not as other Gentiles walk" – the culture of our Gentile brethren is not to be brought into our practice. We are not to walk in the same culture and actions that the rest of the Gentile world walks in. The wickedness that the world practices is not to be our practice. The thinking that they engage in is not to be our thinking. The actions that are justified among the Gentile people, our brethren here in America – it is not acceptable to the believer. We are to leave the American culture and enter into the culture of Christ. Race matters none in regard to the Christian culture. Gentile cultures are divided by racial divides. There is a distinct white American culture, a distinct black American culture, a Mexican-American culture, an American Indian culture, an Asian-American culture within our culture at large. But it doesn't matter if you are white or black or Mexican or Asian; God has rejected the variations of our Gentile cultures and has said, "You must leave it and come into my culture." God accepts no other culture into His. Paul said, "Walk not as other Gentiles walk." God rejects the cultures of this world. He rejects the differences and the similarities that they have and says, "If you want to be my child, if you want to have my blessing, leave the old culture behind and begin to walk in my culture instead."

In America, in days gone by, when people immigrated here, they by and large left their old culture; and they had the thought that they wanted instead to be American. There was a distinct American culture. The rise of multiculturalistic teaching and a preference to the divergence of culture within the borders of America gave rise to the division of America. Diversity does not unify; it divides – to the point that now we have many sub groups within our nation, and all are crying out for greater authority and power. Rather than having unity, we have division within our nation. However, division is not a Scriptural principle. And God says, "You cannot bring your old walk into my culture. You must reject your old walk and the walk of the other Gentiles around you, and you must begin to live by my cultural teaching. You must walk as I walk and reject walking like the rest of the world walks." It is a vast difference. When we do that, however, there is a spiritual unity and identity that comes upon those who reject the worldly culture and cling to God's. God's culture is defined by His Word; what you might consider to be Christian culture is often not Christian at all, but rather just moralized Americanism. God's culture is one of separation from worldliness and clinging to holiness. God's culture is one of obedience to His commands and grace. Wherever in the world there are people who have chosen to follow God's Word in truth and reject the lies of their own cultures, you will find that there is a distinct similarity to the culture that develops; and we are able to gather together in common practice of the faith, no matter where it is that we are.

Paul then begins to make a very scathing indictment of the Gentile cultures. He gives 8 charges against the Gentile cultures that are contrary to the Christian culture.

First, Paul condemns vanity - *Webster's Dictionary* gives this definition of vanity: "Inflation of mind upon slight grounds; empty pride, inspired by an overweening conceit of one's personal attainments or decorations." Paul says that the Gentiles walk in the vanity of their mind. We think that we are great. We have all these things that we have accomplished; we have the grand pomp and platitudes of worldly attainment, and we laud ourselves over our greatness. We want to believe that we are the best at everything. We are the strongest, the fastest, the smartest, the best-looking. There is a natural tendency in the Gentile peoples to exert dominance over others and try to prove their superiority.

There is no doubt that is the American culture. We are vain, we are lifted up in our thinking, and we are out to prove that we are number one. Paul says that the Christian culture is the opposite of that. Here is the summation of the Christian culture on this issue - Philippians 2:3, "Let nothing be done through strife or vainglory; but in lowliness of mind let each esteem other better than themselves." The Christian is to have a humble mind rather than a vain mind. We are to follow in the example of our Saviour in Philippians 2:5-8, "Let this mind be in you, which was also in Christ Jesus: Who, being in the form of God, thought it not robbery to be equal with God:

But made himself of no reputation, and took upon him the form of a servant, and was made in the likeness of men: And being found in fashion as a man, he humbled himself, and became obedient unto death, even the death of the cross."

The old man's understanding is darkened - this means that the concept of living is beyond the understanding of the lost Gentile. It makes no sense to them at all. It is like peering into the darkness and not being able to discern what is there. There is no clarity for them. That which the lost Gentile does not understand, he mocks and seeks to destroy. Every man has a darkened understanding until Christ intervenes. Luke 24:44-45 says, "And he said unto them, These are the words which I spake unto you, while I was yet with you, that all things must be fulfilled, which were written in the law of Moses, and in the prophets, and in the psalms, concerning me. Then opened he their understanding, that they might understand the scriptures." I see the concept of a darkened understanding in my children when we work on their homework. They have a mental block on something, and their mother or I will try to explain it; and we will work at trying to illustrate it. But often it is a struggle, until all at once the light comes on, and they see it. You can see the change in their countenance when that happens; there is an expression that changes on their face, their furrowed brow raises, their eyes open wider, and are enlightened by the understanding. Spirit the lost are in a state of darkness. Don't think it strange that they don't understand; they cannot understand until God gives them light. That is why the propagation of the Scriptures is so important. Psalm 119:130 tells us, "The entrance of thy words giveth light; it giveth understanding unto the simple."

The old man is full of ignorance - this is lack of knowledge. The *Webster's 1828* says, "Ignorance is preferable to error." In other words, it is better to know nothing, than to know something that isn't so. It is harder to un-teach someone than to give them first instruction. Ignorance is not stupidity; it is lack of proper education. A young child is ignorant of many things until they are properly taught. The problem with ignorance is that it is often complicated by vanity; and in that case, the person becomes unteachable, because they are confident in their ignorance, and that becomes stupidity. The Bible says that the ignorance that the Gentiles face is that it alienates us from the life of God. We are dead in trespasses and sin, but we don't know it. We are ignorant of the fact. That fact must be pointed out to us; we have to be taught the law of God, and then have it applied to our hearts, before we can escape the ignorance of our nature. That is why the devil works so hard to rid our culture of the Ten Commandments. That is why the Bible has been removed from the school house and the Ten

Commandments from the court house. Because of the ignorance of the Gentiles and the vanity of our mind, we believe that we have a better idea than God; and so, in our attempt to enforce our better idea, we must rid others of the knowledge of God's law so that we can enforce our own. We must rid the culture of the knowledge of God so that we can establish our own ideas of right and wrong. The American idea of right and wrong is that it is wrong to have and it is right to take. It is wrong to succeed; it is right to receive. We have that idea because we have removed the word of God from our culture. But let's be clear – this is the same problem that has always been present in the Gentile cultures. Paul faced a great battle of ignorance because of this. The Gentiles don't understand life in God because they do not know that they are dead in sin. It is our job to educate them to the truth of the Word of God so that He can teach them the truth about sin and death.

The old man is hindered with blindness. The progression of problems is moving forward here; it began with the vanity of the mind, which produces darkness of the understanding and ignorance of the truth. Now the problem of our culture moves into the area of the heart, and we have a blinded heart. The word *blindness* here literally means "callousness." It means that there is a scale over the heart so

that it cannot perceive as it ought to. Just as in the
eye there can be a cataract that forms and prevents
the vision, there is a layer of callous that forms over
the heart of Gentiles; and it prevents them from per-
ceiving the problems that they have. It vexes their
soul, just as Lot was vexed; and the Bible says how
this happened. 2 Peter 2:7-8 says, "And delivered
just Lot, vexed with the filthy conversation of the
wicked: (For that righteous man dwelling among
them, in seeing and hearing, vexed his righteous
soul from day to day with their unlawful deeds;)".
Lot became blind to the truth, even as a believer in
God, because he was involved in the wickedness of
the heathen. And day by day he became blind to
the problem. The more that you are around sin, the
less that it bothers you and the less that you see it.
I promise you that your television is blinding your
heart. The more that you watch it, the more that
what you see is acceptable, to the point that you
will recommend things as being good that are filled
with filth. Has someone ever told you, "This movie
is good; there is not cursing in it," only to find out
upon watching it that the first five minutes are filled
with vile language and situations? That is because
they had become blind to it. Their heart did not
perceive it because they have been too involved in
the practice of it. There are many who have become
blind in their hearts to the cultural wickedness

around them, because they have involved themselves in the entertainment of the Gentiles.

The old man is past feeling - before long it moves
from simple blindness to the point that we can no
longer even feel guilt over the practices that we are
involved in. The progression of this cultural destruction is amazing. Little by little, the callous is
built upon the heart, first causing blindness to the
problem, and then causing us ultimately to not even
feel guilt when we engage in it ourselves. When you
first saw that thing on the television, you felt bad
about watching it; but you justified it by saying that
at least you weren't doing it. But little by little, you
became blind to that and you don't even really notice it any longer; and now you have come to the
place that you engage in the same actions yourself
and don't feel bad about that either, because your
heart has been thoroughly vexed with sin. The nature of the Gentile culture is to vex the heart and
pave the way to wickedness and destruction through
the continual exposure to sin.

All of this leads the old man to lasciviousness
- *Webster's 1828* says this is "looseness; irregular
indulgence of animal desires; wantonness; lustful-
ness." In other words, it is the tendency to excite
lust and promote irregular indulgences. Listen to
how the word is used in other passages - 2 Corinthians 12:21 says, "*And* lest, when I come again, my

God will humble me among you, and that I shall be-
wail many which have sinned already, and have not
repented of the uncleanness and fornication and
lasciviousness which they have committed." 1 Peter
4:3 says, "For the time past of our life may suffice
us to have wrought the will of the Gentiles, when
we walked in lasciviousness, lusts, excess of wine,
revellings, banquetings, and abominable idolatries."
Lasciviousness seems to be beyond regular fornication, to moving into a more egregious form of perversion. Paul says that the heart of the Gentile can
be so vexed that we feel nothing when engaged in
the most vial forms of wickedness. We live in a time
that our children are so given over to this type of
Gentile culture, murder, sexual immorality; acting
as an animal and upon animal type desires is not
thought to be strange, but normal. That was the
point of the Kinsey report all those years ago. Kinsey believed that we were just animals and that, as
animals, any form of sexual diversion was equal, no
matter what it was. He himself was a pedophile; the
vast majority of his research was with pedophiles.
He thought that bestiality and pedophilia and ho-
mosexuality were just as valid an expression of the
sexual desire as the union of a man and a wife in
marriage. The vast majority of his research was with
sex offenders in prison, and it was passed off as the
population in general. But we have proven the Bible

to be right, that the true nature of Gentiles is to de-volve into the basest forms of wickedness. As our hearts are exposed to more and more debauchery, we as a culture find the most horrific forms of sinful expression acceptable.

Ultimately the old man moves toward complete uncleanness - Paul says that it comes to the point that the Gentile culture is given over to work all uncleanness. There isn't anything that is off limits to the imagination of the mind, once it is rid of the knowledge of God, and the heart is properly vexed to accept the perversion of God's plan for marriage; and we as a nation have crossed over the precipice of this time. We do not live in a Christian culture; we live in the full expression of the Gentile culture that we see expressed here by Paul. There is noth-ing that will not be acceptable in our culture in the future; but take heart – there is hope, because that is the same culture that Paul was preaching to. It is, however, vital that we as believers recognize it be-fore it is too late and we have vexed ourselves with the same uncleanness.

Finally the old man is given over to greediness. He isn't talking about just the corporate fat cats; he is saying that all of our culture is an exercise in greed. We have a lust to have things. The person on welfare is just as guilty of greed as the corporate banker; they just want things that others work for without having to work for it themselves. The politician is greedy of power and money. The culture of greed is part of the nature of the Gentiles; it will not change, no matter who is in office or who is in control. It stands in opposition to the Christian culture, which is a culture of giving. That is not to say that there are not many illustrations of people using religion to fulfill their own greedy lusts. This is not a condemnation to Christianity; it is rather proof that the old man is ever present, and men will use whatever means necessary to accomplish their sinful desires. Men who walk in the old nature, whether lost or saved, are prone to the same sinful lusts. We are told to come out of this wicked culture of greed and uncleanness. We are told to stop walking as the Gentiles walk. That is a startling thought – that we, if we are not cautious, can find ourselves walking in that wicked culture and not even know it.

The old man is corrupt and brings destruction and misery to life. It is vital that we put off the old man with his deeds, and in the next chapter we will see the pattern that God gives us for doing just that.

CHAPTER 6

The Put Off / Put On Process

Ephesians 4:20-24 "But ye have not so learned Christ; If so be that ye have heard him, and have been taught by him, as the truth is in Jesus: That ye put off concerning the former conversation the old man, which is corrupt according to the deceitful lusts; And be renewed in the spirit of your mind; And that ye put on the new man, which after God is created in righteousness and true holiness."

In Chapter Five we saw the character of the old Gentile nature that we have. It isn't a pretty picture. The old nature is full of vanity and pride; it is darkened in the understanding, ignorant of the life that is in God, blinded in the heart, given to lasciviousness, working all uncleanness, and greedy. By comparison, the new nature which we have in Christ is the complete opposite. It is humble, enlightened in understanding, filled with the knowledge of God, obedient in the heart, given to holiness, working all righteousness, and giving.

If you are saved, you have been transformed by the saving blood of Jesus Christ. The old nature is not gone, but we now have a new option for living. The old man is still present, but we now can learn to walk in the Spirit rather than in the flesh. That is the key to this process that we see here. The learning element is often overlooked. We get saved, and we want the old nature to just vanish. We want never have to deal with it again, and we don't want to have to learn to do differently. That is how God presents the contrast here, however. Listen again to what it says in Ephesians 4:20-21: "But ye have not so learned Christ; If so be that ye have heard him, and have been taught by him, as the truth is in Jesus:" God is in the process of teaching you in the truth by Jesus Christ. If you have received Him, He is in you, and you can hear Him teach you. Jesus said in John 10:27, "My sheep hear my voice, and I know them, and they follow me:"

The new nature in essence is this: when you got saved, God moved into your heart; and He is speaking to you to teach you how to resist the old sinful nature and walk in a way that is pleasing to Him. The issue is learning to listen and obey His voice in your heart. He is speaking, but sometimes we don't listen. He is teaching, but sometimes we don't learn. The actual process of teaching is three-fold according to this passage.

Ephesians 4:22-24 "That ye put off concerning the former conversation the old man, which is corrupt according to the deceitful lusts; And be renewed in the spirit of your mind; And that ye put on the new man, which after God is created in righteousness and true holiness."

Notice here the three-step process of learning to walk in the new nature. First, identify the old man actions – before you can do that which is right, you must first identify that which is wrong and needs to be removed. Often, we want to skip step one and two in this process and just add the new things without removing the old. Paul says that these old things are divided into two categories: former conversations and deceitful lusts.

Former conversations are the things that are habitual in our nature. These are the things that we often don't even recognize as being there or being a problem. When we see them we are shocked, because they are not necessarily conscious actions, but rather our default way of acting. These things come naturally to the flesh and are the earmarks of our sinful nature that are often hard to root out and correct, because they have become besetting sins in our life.

Deceitful lusts are the lusts we have justified in our life. We have been deceived by them and believe either that they are necessary or that we are incapable of ridding ourselves of them. The word *deceitful* literally means "delusional." A person who is given to the lust of alcohol is under the delusion that they don't have a problem, or that they cannot function without it, or some other delusion. The person who is given to adulteries is under the delusion that it doesn't hurt anyone and it is just an outlet for their needs, or some other lie that they have bought into.

Before a person can move forward in walking in the new nature, the old nature must be identified. The old man must be pointed out. This process of illuminating the old nature occurs through attendance to the Word of God. Psalm 119:105 tells us, "Thy word is a lamp unto my feet, and a light unto my path." Psalm 119:130 says, "The entrance of thy words giveth light; it giveth understanding unto the simple. As we as believers read God's Word, the Spirit of God within us takes it and shines His light upon the old sinful deeds and reveals the places that we are deceived. Simply knowing where we are deceived or what old sinful actions we were doing is not the end of the process; it is the beginning. It begins the process by producing conviction in our hearts and driving us to seek a remedy for the problem.

The second step that Paul teaches us is to renew the mind. The word *renew* means "to renovate"; it means to take out the old way of thinking and install a new way of thinking. How do we renew our thinking? Colossians 3:10 says, "And have put on the new man, which is renewed in knowledge after the image of him that created him." We must begin to search the Scriptures and seek the knowledge of Him to replace the deceitful lusts that have pervaded our thoughts. We will discuss this more farther in the book.

Finally, we must put on the new man actions. We have identified the old man actions and determined to put them off; we have searched our thinking to correct the wrong thinking that had lead to the sinful actions, and corrected that thinking with the Word of God; so then we begin to act accordingly to the will of God in walking in the truth. Putting on the new man actions is the natural result of changing our sinful thinking to righteous thinking. Paul gives many illustrations to show this process in the rest of this chapter.

Illustrated by the sin of lying - Ephesians 4:25 says, "Wherefore putting away lying, speak every man truth with his neighbour: for we are members one of another."

1. The old man action - lying
2. The new man action - speaking the truth
3. The correction of the deceit in thinking - we are members one of another

Illustrated by sinful anger - Ephesians 4:26-27 tells us, "Be ye angry, and sin not: let not the sun go down upon your wrath: Neither give place to the devil."

1. The old man action - sinful anger
2. The new man action - dealing with anger immediately
3. The correction of the deceit in thinking - we were giving place to the devil

Illustrated by stealing - Ephesians 4:28 says, "Let him that stole steal no more: but rather let him labour, working with his hands the thing which is good, that he may have to give to him that needeth."

1. The old man action - stealing
2. The new man action - working and giving
3. The correction of the deceit in thinking – Others have needs that we can fill

Illustrated by corrupt communication - Ephesians 4:29-30 says, "Let no corrupt communication proceed out of your mouth, but that which is good to the use of edifying, that it may minister grace unto the hearers. And grieve not the holy Spirit of God, whereby ye are sealed unto the day of redemption."

1. The old man action - speaking corrupt (rotten or worthless) communication
2. The new man action - speaking good things to edify and minister grace
3. The correction of the deceit in thinking – How we speak matters to God - Matthew 12:36 says, "But I say unto you, That every idle word that men shall speak, they shall give

account thereof in the day of judgment."

Illustrated by a host of other sinful things and righteous actions - Ephesians 4:31-32 "Let all bitterness, and wrath, and anger, and clamour, and evil speaking, be put away from you, with all malice: And be ye kind one to another, tenderhearted, forgiving one another, even as God for Christ's sake hath forgiven you."

1. The old man action - bitterness, wrath, anger clamour, evil speaking
2. The new man action - kindness, tenderhearted, forgiveness
3. The correction of the deceit in thinking - God has already forgiven you

You see the process is the same no matter what the sin is. Let the Word of God search out the sinful actions, correct the deceitful thinking that lead to that action, and put on the new and spiritually opposite action that God has shown in His Word.

Day by day we are learning to walk in the new nature. We must always remember that it is a learning process. We are learning new lessons about our spiritual walk every day, and every day God is shedding His light in our hearts to reveal the old deceits and begin the process of change in us that will produce Godliness and holiness in our lives.

CHAPTER 7

Discerning the Wiles of the Devil to Trap You

The Bible warns us that we are in a spiritual warfare; this battle covers a wide area of conflict, ranging from the old nature within us and our old carnal thinking, to an adversary who the Bible describes as an accuser and a roaring lion, the devil. While it is fair to say that you are often your own worst enemy, your old nature is definitely not your only enemy. Paul said in Ephesians 6:12, "For we wrestle not against flesh and blood, but against principalities, against powers, against the rulers of the darkness of this world, against spiritual wickedness in high places."

Any truly Biblical study on overcoming the pitfalls of sin in our lives must include getting an understanding of both of the enemies of righteousness – the flesh and the devil. To understand this enemy you must know some things about him. The Bible teaches us all that we need to know about the devil, in showing us the way that he works, through naming him by his wicked actions.

The first thing we see about the devil in the Bible is that he is intent on deceiving people and luring them into sin. The account of the devil's first interaction with people is found in **Genesis 3:1-7**. There we see the tactic of Satan as he twists the Word of God to bring confusion to Eve and deceive her. It says there, "Now the serpent was more subtil than any beast of the field which the LORD God had made. And he said unto the woman, Yea, hath God said, Ye shall not eat of every tree of the garden? And the woman said unto the serpent, We may eat of the fruit of the trees of the garden: But of the fruit of the tree which is in the midst of the garden, God hath said, Ye shall not eat of it, neither shall ye touch it, lest ye die. And the serpent said unto the woman, Ye shall not surely die: For God doth know that in the day ye eat thereof, then your eyes shall be opened, and ye shall be as gods, knowing good and evil. And when the woman saw that the tree was good for food, and that it was pleasant to the eyes, and a tree to be desired to make one wise, she took of the fruit thereof, and did eat, and gave also unto her husband with her; and he did eat. And the eyes of them both were opened, and they knew that they were naked; and they sewed fig leaves together, and made themselves aprons."

Notice how the first thing that Satan does is put a negative slant on the commandment of God. The commandment was for life. God said, "Don't eat of this tree, or it will bring death"; yet the devil twisted it to be a limit to their happiness. If God would just allow you to do all the things that you want to do, you could be happy; but He has limited you, He has withheld true joy from you. The second thing that we see the devil do here is to straight up deny the truth. He told Eve, "Ye shall not surely die." He lied to her! In her innocence, she believed the lie of the devil over the warning of God. Paul said in 1 Timothy 2:14, "And Adam was not deceived, but the woman being deceived was in the transgression." Adam sinned willfully to remain with Eve, but Eve was deceived into sin. The devil works relentlessly to deceive and pervert the minds of people to cause them to sin, because he knows that **Romans 6:23** is true when it says, "The wages of sin is death." Jesus identified the devil as a murderer and a liar in John 8:44 when He said, "Ye are of your father the devil, and the lusts of your father ye will do. He was a murderer from the beginning, and abode not in the truth, because there is no truth in him. When he speaketh a lie, he speaketh of his own: for he is a liar, and the father of it."

Satan is a liar and uses his lies to draw people into sin and destruction, so that they reap the wages of sin in their lives, death, thus making him a murderer. In the end Satan will be defeated and his lies exposed for what they are. It says in Revelation

12:9-10, "And the great dragon was cast out, that old serpent, called the Devil, and Satan, which deceiveth the whole world: he was cast out into the earth, and his angels were cast out with him. And I heard a loud voice saying in heaven, Now is come salvation, and strength, and the kingdom of our God, and the power of his Christ: for the accuser of our brethren is cast down, which accused them before our God day and night." In this passage we see the devil identified as the one which deceiveth the whole world. The Devil has spread his lies to every person on the earth; there is no one who has not been infected and affected by the lies of Satan.

There is also another title given here that identifies the way that the Devil works; he is called the accuser. The devil works hard to bring accusation about believers continually, the Bible said here, day and night. He never rests from his disgusting work. The book of Job is an example of this accusatory work of Satan. It tells us in Job 1:6-11, "Now there was a day when the sons of God came to present themselves before the LORD, and Satan came also among them. And the LORD said unto Satan, Whence comest thou? Then Satan answered the LORD, and said, From going to and fro in the earth, and from walking up and down in it. And the LORD said unto Satan, Hast thou considered my servant Job, that there is none like him in the earth, a perfect

and an upright man, one that feareth God, and es-
cheweth evil? Then Satan answered the LORD, and
said, Doth Job fear God for nought? Hast not thou
made an hedge about him, and about his house,
and about all that he hath on every side? thou hast
blessed the work of his hands, and his substance is
increased in the land. But put forth thine hand now,
and touch all that he hath, and he will curse thee to
thy face." Satan is constantly on the prowl to find
some believer who is faltering, whom he can bring
accusations against.

Peter said it this way in 1 Peter 5:8: "Be sober, be vigilant; because your adversary the devil,
as a roaring lion, walketh about, seeking whom he
may devour." He is a liar, a murderer, an accuser,
and without a doubt our adversary as he seeks to
hinder our walk with God; and the way that he has
found to be most effective is in this area of telling
lies and affecting our thinking. For this cause, we
are warned repeatedly to beware of the devil; yet I
find that many times we are blindly walking around
with no armor on to protect us from his dastardly
designs. We are warned in Ephesians 6:11 to "Put
on the whole armour of God, that ye may be able to
stand against the wiles of the devil." The word *wiles*
means "to lie in wait to trick." It means the traps that
he has set, the snares and nets that he has laid in our
path, hoping to catch us not watching, so that we

might stumble into sin. Several times this warning is given in the Scriptures concerning the snares of the devil. Paul said to Timothy concerning a pastor in 1 Timothy 3:7, "Moreover he must have a good report of them which are without; lest he fall into reproach and the snare of the devil." Even pastors can be caught in the snare of the devil if they are not careful watching against his wiles. Paul said again in 2 Timothy 2:26, "And that they may recover themselves out of the snare of the devil, who are taken captive by him at his will."

We are to be constantly aware; the Bible uses the term *watch* to describe how we are to walk in this world, being attentive to the fact that we know Satan has laid snares to trap us. Jesus told His disciples in Mark 14:38, "Watch ye and pray, lest ye enter into temptation. The spirit truly is ready, but the flesh is weak." And Paul warned us in 1 Thessalonians 5:6, "Therefore let us not sleep, as do others; but let us watch and be sober." In many other places as well, we are cautioned to be watchful, knowing that the enemy is at work, trying to catch us in the trap of his lies. The great news is that we are told in Proverbs 1:17, "Surely in vain the net is spread in the sight of any bird." If we are watching, we are less likely to be caught up in the trap; if we are attentive, we have a greater chance of seeing the snare and avoiding the lies that the devil has been telling us. We do not have to allow Satan to have victory over us, because Paul told us in 2 Corinthians 2:11, "Lest Satan should get an advantage of us: for we are not ignorant of his devices. We know how he works; we have been given the outline of his plan in the Bible. That doesn't mean that we will never be caught in a snare; it means that we don't have to be caught if we are attentive and obedient to the Word of God.

In addition to being a liar, murderer, accuser, and our adversary, the Bible shows us that the devil is a tempter. He knows the weaknesses of your flesh and seeks to exploit them. He even tried this with Jesus, and over an eleven verse passage, we see Jesus do spiritual battle with the tempter. Matthew 4:1-11 says, "Then was Jesus led up of the Spirit into the wilderness to be tempted of the devil. And when he had fasted forty days and forty nights, he was afterward an hungered. And when the tempter came to him, he said, If thou be the Son of God, command that these stones be made bread. But he answered and said, It is written, Man shall not live by bread alone, but by every word that proceedeth out of the mouth of God. Then the devil taketh him up into the holy city, and setteth him on a pinnacle of the temple, And saith unto him, If thou be the Son of God, cast thyself down: for it is written, He shall give his angels charge concerning thee: and in their hands they shall bear thee up, lest at any time thou dash thy foot against a stone. Jesus said unto him, It is written again, Thou shalt not tempt the Lord thy God. Again, the devil taketh him up into an exceeding high mountain, and sheweth him all the kingdoms of the world, and the glory of them; And saith unto him, All these things will I give thee, if thou wilt fall down and worship me. Then saith Jesus unto him, Get thee hence, Satan: for it is written, Thou shalt worship the Lord thy God, and him only shalt thou serve. Then the devil leaveth him, and, behold, angels came and ministered unto him."

Three times the tempter tries to lure Jesus into sin, by tempting Him with the lust of the flesh, the lust of the eyes, and the pride of life. John said this is the sum of all sin in 1 John 2:16: "For all that is in the world, the lust of the flesh, and the lust of the eyes, and the pride of life, is not of the Father, but is of the world." The answer to these temptations was the same each time, "It is written." Satan doesn't have to tempt the lost with these things, because they are wholly given over to fulfill the lust of the old man already. It is the believer that he tempts, to derail them from being useful to God. Paul said in 1 Thessalonians 3:5, "For this cause, when I could no longer forbear, I sent to know your faith, lest by some means the tempter have tempted you, and our labour be in vain." Paul knew the tempter well; he had been afflicted by him more than once. He had seen others drawn away, such as Demas, who forsook him because he loved this present world and was prey to the work of the tempter.

The devil works against people on three levels. The first is against the lost man, whom he can posses to do his work. Many times in the Gospels, we see Jesus doing spiritual battle with the devil over his possession of the lost. It says in Matthew 9:32, "As they went out, behold, they brought to him a dumb man possessed with a devil." The possession of an individual can affect their soul and their body. They will say and do what the devil bids them to do if they are possessed of him. One of the illustrations in the Bible of this is Mark 5:2-5: "And when he was come out of the ship, immediately there met him out of the tombs a man with an unclean spirit, Who had his dwelling among the tombs; and no man could bind him, no, not with chains: Because that he had been often bound with fetters and chains, and the chains had been plucked asunder by him, and the fetters broken in pieces: neither could any man tame him. And always, night and day, he was in the mountains, and in the tombs, crying, and cutting himself with stones."

There are other illustrations of what the devil does to people when he possesses them; but the good news is that the Devil is subject to God, and when he is removed by Jesus Christ, the person is free from His bondage in their mind and body in this way. Matthew 17:18 illustrates this when it says, "And Jesus rebuked the devil; and he departed out of him: and the child was cured from that very hour."

The next level that the devil can work is in oppression. Acts 10:38 says, "How God anointed Jesus of Nazareth with the Holy Ghost and with power: who went about doing good, and healing all that were oppressed of the devil; for God was with him." Now a believer cannot be possessed, because God will not share His glory. However, a believer can be oppressed, as seen in the account of Paul's physical affliction in 2 Corinthians 12:7: "And lest I should be exalted above measure through the abundance of the revelations, there was given to me a thorn in the flesh, the messenger of Satan to buffet me, lest I should be exalted above measure." The oppression of the enemy can be physical or on a spiritual level, as he attacks and seeks to hinder us from serving God. Many times in the book of Acts, the apostles faced the spiritual oppression of the devil as he used the rulers to seek to prohibit them from speaking of Jesus. They were cast into prison and beaten; they were abused in body, soul, and spirit to seek to turn them aside from preaching the truth. The oppressor was hard at work to try and hinder them from doing the work of God.

The final level that we see in the Bible concerning the work of Satan is that if he cannot posses or oppress, he will seek to obsess us with him, so that we stop doing what God has called us to do. This is very clearly seen in Acts 16:16-18: "And it came to pass, as we went to prayer, a certain damsel possessed with a spirit of divination met us, which brought her masters much gain by soothsaying: The same followed Paul and us, and cried, saying, These men are the servants of the most high God, which shew unto us the way of salvation. And this did she many days. But Paul, being grieved, turned and said to the spirit, I command thee in the name of Jesus Christ to come out of her. And he came out the same hour." Here we see a woman who was possessed of the devil and was being used to try and get the attention of the apostles off what they were to do and onto her. He wanted to get them obsessed with what he could do. For many days he attempted this, until finally Paul said, "We will not allow you to divert our attention," and through the name of Jesus Christ cast the devil out of the woman. There are some who become obsessed with seeing what the devil is doing. Rather than moving forward in the things that God has given them to do, they are constantly looking at what the devil is doing.

The enemy is shrewd and will use any tactic that he can to divert us from the work of God and from walking with God. Matthew 13:39 says, "The enemy that sowed them is the devil; the harvest is the end of the world; and the reapers are the angels." The devil has sown many people, even in churches, to hinder the work of God. There are people who claim to be believers but are not; they are deceivers and liars planted to hinder you from God's work. One of the ways you can know the difference between a believer and a pretender is by their works. 1 John 3:8 says, "He that committeth sin is of the devil; for the devil sinneth from the beginning. For this purpose the Son of God was manifested, that he might destroy the works of the devil." That does not mean that a believer will be sinless, but a person who lives in sin and seeks to encourage others to do so while claiming to be a believer is a liar.

You need to know that, though the devil is a skilled and accomplished adversary, you don't have to be in fear of him, only watchful for his attacks. We are told in 1 John 4:4, "Ye are of God, little children, and have overcome them: because greater is he that is in you, than he that is in the world." We are more than conquerors thorough Jesus Christ who lives within us. The devil has a certain end awaiting him as it tells us in Matthew 25:41, "Then shall he say also unto them on the left hand, Depart from me, ye cursed, into everlasting fire, prepared for the devil and his angels." There is a place prepared for the devil and all those who have followed his example of not being obedient to the Lord Jesus Christ. His end is already determined; and his fate is described in Revelation 20:10, "And the devil that deceived them was cast into the lake of fire and brimstone, where the beast and the false prophet are, and shall be tormented day and night for ever and ever."

In the mean time, we are given the commandment to watch. We are told in Ephesians 4:27, "Neither give place to the devil." That means that we are not to allow ourselves to be caught up in his snares. If we find ourselves there, we have the weapons to be freed because the blood of Jesus Christ cleanseth us from all sin. What we must do is follow the admonition of James 4:7: "Submit yourselves therefore to God. Resist the devil, and he will flee from you."

The battle that you face against the flesh and your adversary the Devil is one that has already been won by the blood of Jesus Christ; yet daily we must apply the victory to our lives, through attentively watching for the snares and wiles of the Devil and avoiding them. The process of becoming attentive to the snares is not difficult. We have already seen in Proverbs 1:17, "Surely in vain the net is spread in the sight of any bird." I encourage you to begin what I call a trigger list to give you the practice of identifying the snares in your life. A trigger is something that activates the desire to commit sin. Often, the addict will seem to be doing well at maintaining freedom from their sin; and then seemingly out of nowhere their thinking is drawn into the abyss of destruction, and before they know it they are back involved in the sin. They are caught as a bird in a snare; they did not see it coming, and they are devastated about it but feel helpless. You are not helpless; you must however identify the process that is taking place.

A large part of this process of identifying the snares and wiles of the Devil is explained in 2 Corinthians 10:4-6: "(For the weapons of our warfare are not carnal, but mighty through God to the pulling down of strong holds;) Casting down imaginations, and every high thing that exalteth itself against the knowledge of God, and bringing into captivity every thought to the obedience of Christ; And having in a readiness to revenge all disobedience, when your obedience is fulfilled." The Scriptures here define a three-part process that is vital if we are going to gain victory over the thought snares of the devil; we are going to call them the 3 C's.

The first step is **casting** down imaginations. The snares of the devil are often triggered in the thought life and incubate in our mind, the lust of the old man. If I am going to have victory over the sin that has beset me I must begin with stopping it at the

imagination stage.   There must be a firm commit-
ment in your heart not to allow the thought to go
forward, to grab it with a fervency and cast it out.
To allow it to stay is tantamount to sitting on the
couch and watching someone rob your house until
you get the courage to stand up and say stop. The
likelihood is that if you stay silent about it, he will
steal you blind; the longer you sit in silence, the less
likely you are to actually get up and stop the travesty.

The second step is **capturing** the wrong thought
and examining its source. The Scriptures say, "Bring
that thought into captivity." I encourage you to
keep a small note pad with you all the time; and as
soon as your thinking starts to go astray, stop and
ask yourself, "What just happened?" It may have
been an event, it may have been a comment by
someone, it may have been a place that you passed,
or even a smell or color; it could be any number of
things that you have allowed the devil to attach to
your thinking, that bring back the memories of sin
in your heart. They trigger the lie and plunge you
into the wrong thinking again that will lead to the
wrong action if it is followed. The trigger list is a
way of watching and keeping yourself aware that
the devil has laid snares for you. As soon as you are
blindly walking along, you will be prey again to him.
Determining the source of the errant thinking will
help you to walk back out of the detrimental think-

ing process and move back into the right thinking. It is saying to Satan, "I will not let you grab control of my thinking and thus snare me in a trap of sin."

A trigger list may look like this:

7/2/12

10:45 am - thought about how good a beer would taste right now - I just walked by the beer cooler in the store

11:20 am - remembered a party that I was at a few months ago - I saw someone wearing a corona shirt

11:50 am - started to think about drink mixes - smelled some citrus smell

When you have that imagination come into your thinking, stop! Say within yourself, "I will not indulge this; I reject this thought." Then take out your trigger list and record it, along with the thing that happened which might have triggered you to think the damaging thought. The day and time are a good thing to record, because you might find that you have more trouble on certain days or at certain times as you develop your list more. You also might find that certain senses trigger more thoughts than others. A trigger may be anything around you – it could be sights, smells, sounds, songs, certain people, or people dressed a certain way. You may not be able to eliminate all these things from happening around you; but if you are aware of the link, you can begin to sever the tie that those things have on your thinking.

The third and final step in this process is **correcting** the thinking pattern that was leading down the road to sin. The Bible said we were to have a readiness to revenge all disobedience; thus we are looking for the things that we have done in our past that have laid the point of Satan's snare. The wrong actions of our past have given him many places to tie us to. Proverbs 5:22 says, "His own iniquities shall take the wicked himself, and he shall be holden with the cords of his sins." These cords are the triggers that Satan uses to lay the traps for our thinking. When you have taken the steps of casting down the sinful imagination and then capturing the sinful thinking to determine its sources, the third process of correcting the thinking pattern can be accomplished by following the process of Biblical fasting, assuming that you are already saved. You must cut the cords of iniquity that gave Satan the opportunity to set a snare for your thinking. You are taking back the ground that you have yielded to him in this way and cutting the cords of iniquity that are attached to the trigger. One by one you can cut the triggers and gain freedom, but every believer should maintain awareness of the fact that the adversary is busy day and night seeking whom he may devour. Your attention to your path is vital if you are going to have victory over him.

Eliminating the triggers and avoiding the snares is an important step in gaining victory in your life, but it is not the only thing that you must do to win the battle over deceitful thinking and sinful actions. The process of putting on the new man and putting off the old man has just begun at this point.

CHAPTER 8

Exposing the Lies and Renewing the Mind

In order to put off the old man and his deeds, we must spend some time on how to expose the lies that form the wrong beliefs to produce the sinful actions. We have already established that if our actions are wrong, then thinking that we engage in is wrong. The problem is that we must learn where we have believed lies, and that is not always an easy process. If you knew that what you believed was a lie, you wouldn't believe it. Often, the lies are subtle and difficult to root out. The light of the truth is the only torch that can reveal what lies have been embedded in your thinking.

The issue is our darkened thinking. Our old man operates under a veil of darkness; the old man has no spiritual light and even hates the light. The light of God was revealed in Jesus Christ. John unveiled this truth when he said in John 1:5, "And the light shineth in darkness; and the darkness comprehended it not." The lost man does not comprehend how Jesus Christ is the light. Our concept of light is as a physical light, but we fail to comprehend the spiritual light that is Jesus Christ. It is this spiritual darkness that condemns us; as John 3:19 tells us, "And this is the condemnation, that light is come into the world, and men loved darkness rather than light, because their deeds were evil." Our evil deeds are the result of our darkened hearts. When Jesus Christ comes into the heart through salvation, He brings His light into your life; and the light of His Word becomes illuminated by His presence. When we are saved, His light dwells in us; but to have His light be the illumination that He wants it to be, we must follow Him. John 8:12 says, "Then spake Jesus again unto them, saying, I am the light of the world: he that followeth me shall not walk in darkness, but shall have the light of life." The lost man or wayward believer has a difficult time because he do not see where his path is leading. In John 12:35 Jesus told us, "Then Jesus said unto them, Yet a little while is the light with you. Walk while ye have the light, lest darkness come upon you: for he that walketh in darkness knoweth not whither he goeth."

The issue in our thinking is as clear as light and darkness. Our old nature hates the light and loves the lies. As long as our thinking is done in the darkness, the lies have a place of refuge; but when we shed the light on our thinking, it begins to expose the lies for what they are. When the light is shed abroad in our heart, the lies have no place to hide; and we are able to clean them out. Like so many cobwebs in our mind, the clutter and dust of the old man must be cleaned out of our thinking if we are going to inhabit our bodies in righteousness and the peace of God. David expressed the way that the Word of God works as a light to shine in our hearts and minds. He says in Psalm 119:11, "Thy word have I hid in mine heart, that I might not sin against thee." The Word of God is a bastion against sin when it is hidden in your heart, because it replaces the old nature thinking. David says again in Psalm 119:105, "Thy word is a lamp unto my feet, and a light unto my path." The Word of God provides a light to the path of our actions, because we are able to see clearly through its application in our hearts. Then finally David says in Psalm 119:130, "The entrance of thy words giveth light; it giveth understanding unto the simple." When the Word of God makes its way into your mind and heart, it literally brings with it spiritual light. It will make the simple wise; it will reveal the lies of the darkness and give you the ability to identify them.

The connection between the Word of God and fellowship with God is so strong in the Bible that the effect of being filled with the Spirit in Ephesians 5:18-21 ("And be not drunk with wine, wherein is excess; but be filled with the Spirit; Speaking to yourselves in psalms and hymns and spiritual songs, singing and making melody in your heart to the

Lord; Giving thanks always for all things unto God and the Father in the name of our Lord Jesus Christ; Submitting yourselves one to another in the fear of God") is nearly identical to the effect of being filled with the Word of God in Colossians 3:16-17 ("Let the word of Christ dwell in you richly in all wisdom; teaching and admonishing one another in psalms and hymns and spiritual songs, singing with grace in your hearts to the Lord. And whatsoever ye do in word or deed, do all in the name of the Lord Jesus, giving thanks to God and the Father by him").

You cannot be filled with the Spirit of God unless the Word of God is dwelling in you. Spirituality is not a state of mind; it is a filling of God and His Word. You can act religious and you can do religious things and not be filled with the Spirit of God; but when you are filled with the Word of God and the Spirit of God, you cannot do carnal things. Paul says in Galatians 5:16, "This I say then, Walk in the Spirit, and ye shall not fulfil the lust of the flesh." The truth of God's Word inoculates us against walking in the flesh, if we allow it to dwell in us and we walk in the Spirit. It is amazing how quickly though that a person can move back into the flesh and allow their thinking to turn back to the old man.

The issue is that you must determine to love the truth more than the lies. You have to determine to replace the lies with the truth. David was a man af-

ter God's own heart, because David knew that loving God meant loving the truth of God. You cannot say that you love God and that you don't love
His truth. Over and over again, David showed the
power of the truth in His life.

David recognized that the source of all truth
in his life was from the Word of God. He said in
Psalm 119:30, "I have chosen the way of truth: thy
judgments have I laid before me." Can you say that?
Can you be honest in your heart and say that you
have chosen the way of truth and that you have laid
the judgments (the Word of God) before you as a
guide to your life? Can you say that you have made
the choice to guide each decision in your life by the
principles of the Word of God and refuse walking
in the thinking of your flesh? David recognized
that the only source of truth that there was is God's
Word. All other things start from a human perspective and will lead down the path of lies. He said in
Psalm 119:151, "Thou art near, O LORD; and all
thy commandments are truth." There are times that
we read a statement that seems to resonate with us
as being true. You may have seen a bumper sticker
or a sign that caught your attention and you said,
"That is true." The problem is that sometimes those
things are true and sometimes they are not. The
same thing cannot be said about the Scriptures –
every part of the Bible is true, every phrase and ev-

ery Word is true; there is not some portion that you will come across that you might say is questionable. Every Word of God is true, and all other things are questionable. Paul said in Romans 3:4, "God forbid: yea, let God be true, but every man a liar; as it is written, That thou mightest be justified in thy sayings, and mightest overcome when thou art judged."

The works of God are based upon His Word; that is what we are to do also. David said in Psalm 33:4, "For the word of the LORD is right; and all his works are done in truth." When our works don't line up with His Word, they will be done in lies; but when we align our thinking with His Word, which is right and true, the deeds that follow will be true as well. The issue of God's Word being true is so important to God that He even had David say in Psalm 138:2, "I will worship toward thy holy temple, and praise thy name for thy lovingkindness and for thy truth: for thou hast magnified thy word above all thy name."

David earnestly desired to be led by the truth of God's Word. He begged God in Psalm 25:5, "Lead me in thy truth, and teach me: for thou art the God of my salvation; on thee do I wait all the day." The old man does not understand or know the way of the Lord, and thus it is vital to instill God's Word into the heart if we are going to transform our mind to the obedience of Christ. David prayed in Psalm

86:11, "Teach me thy way, O LORD; I will walk in thy truth: unite my heart to fear thy name."

David knew that God's great desire for him was that truth would be established in him. Psalm 51:6 says, "Behold, thou desirest truth in the inward parts: and in the hidden part thou shalt make me to know wisdom." God didn't have a desire for David to walk in His truth any more than He has that same desire for you to do so. The difference is the level of importance that David obviously placed upon filling His life with God's Word. The difference is that David had recognized that his thinking was faulty and prone to sinfulness and that the Word of God was the only source of absolute truth and spiritual strength. David yielded all of His thinking to God in this way. He wanted his old natural thinking to be overtaken by the truth of the Bible; he wanted the truth to permeate his thinking and thus his actions.

One of the ways that we can see the truth of God's Word being dominant in our thinking is that God's truth always leads us to the fellowship of His house. David said in Psalm 43:3, "O send out thy light and thy truth: let them lead me; let them bring me unto thy holy hill, and to thy tabernacles." When we love the truth, God makes it our protection. Psalm 91:4 says, "He shall cover thee with his feathers, and under his wings shalt thou trust: his truth shall be thy shield and buckler." Without the truth, we are unguarded and unprotected from the attacks of the enemy and from the sinfulness of our flesh. The truth is a shield to deflect the fiery darts of the wicked one. A buckler was a type of shield that was at least four feet tall and was designed to protect the whole body from the attacks of the enemy. God's truth is the only defense that you need against the lies of the flesh and the devil, but you must give it the prominent place that it deserves. If you want to know where the lies are, dive deeply into the Word of God and saturate yourself with the truth.

Solomon said in Proverbs 23:23, "Buy the truth, and sell it not; also wisdom, and instruction, and understanding." The key to illuminating your thinking is to flood it with the truth of God's holy Word. In counseling, I have people begin to do an exercise that is designed to help them begin to shed the light into their thinking and identify lies that have been lying in the darkness. In a note book, place three headings at the top of the page. The first heading is "The Lie"; the second heading is "The Truth"; and the third heading is "The Scripture." Once you have done this, take your Bible and pray as David did in Psalm 119:18, "Open thou mine eyes, that I may behold wondrous things out of thy law." As you read the Scriptures, look for verses that stand out to you and ask this question: "What lie have I heard that contradicts this truth?" Write down the lie, the truth, and the verse on your sheet and continue on. Some of these lies may not seem to be a problem for you; but if you have asked God to show you His light, there is a likelihood that somewhere this lie is affecting your thinking. Day by day, continue this process of identifying the truth and pointing out the lies, and what you will find is that you will begin to see more and more of the lies as your heart and mind are flooded with the truth.

The Lie	The Truth	The Scripture
1. I can get away with sin	Sin always has consequences	Numbers 32:23 But if ye will not do so, behold, ye have sinned against the LORD: and be sure your sin will find you out.
2.		

CHAPTER 9

Putting on the New Man

Exposing the truth gives us the ability to begin to form a new paradigm and replace the old nature responses with righteous substitutions. Remember what we are told in Romans 12:1-2: "I beseech you therefore, brethren, by the mercies of God, that ye present your bodies a living sacrifice, holy, acceptable unto God, which is your reasonable service. And be not conformed to this world: but be ye transformed by the renewing of your mind, that ye may prove what is that good, and acceptable, and perfect, will of God." The actions of the body are changed when our mind is transformed and renewed. The word *renewed* means "to be renovated."

Some time ago, I purchased a house that I foolishly decided I could live in and remodel at the same time, not a plan that I recommend. It was messy and uncomfortable. It was a good illustration of what we are talking about here, however, because the same is true when we are renewing our mind – it is very uncomfortable, and it can be very messy as well. The process in my home went something like this: tear out the old stuff and dispose of it; install the framework for what things would look like in the new space; and then cover them with the sheet rock, mud, and paint. You get the point; you don't just erect new walls without tearing out the old ones. Ultimately the process was accomplished one room at a time. It is important that you grab hold of that concept – you cannot live in a house and tear the whole thing down at the same time; you must take one room at a time and renovate it. We started with the worst rooms first and then worked our way to the rest.

The idea of renovating your mind and thus changing the actions that you have been struggling with demands that new things cover up the old. Jesus gives us an account of someone who only went part way in Matthew 12:43-45: "When the unclean spirit is gone out of a man, he walketh through dry places, seeking rest, and findeth none. Then he saith, I will return into my house from whence I came out; and when he is come, he findeth it empty, swept, and garnished. Then goeth he, and taketh with himself seven other spirits more wicked than himself, and they enter in and dwell there: and the last state of that man is worse than the first. Even so shall it be also unto this wicked generation."

This teaches us that it is not enough to just tear out the old, if we do not put something new back in its place. What we must do is install new habits, new responses, and ultimately new triggers that turn us to right responses instead of the old sinful responses. Triggers themselves are not bad if they bring about right actions. The new triggers are installed to override the old and prevent us from sliding back into the same old sinful actions. We are renewing our mind in such a way. This is not possible until the old lies are exposed and the truth is present in its place, but once that has happened we must begin to establish new and right patterns that will guide our behavior.

This process can be seen illustrated in many areas of our life. I remember hearing of athletes that were trying to make improvements to their abilities, such as golfers who were learning a new swing, or quarterbacks who were learning a new throwing motion. They had to correct the defect that was in their natural thinking and train themselves to operate in a new way. That is similar to what we must do in a spiritual sense when it comes to the old and new nature. We must identify what the defects in our actions are and what thinking has led to this problem, then we learn a new way of thinking to produce a new action that is honoring to God. That is the renewing of the mind process; it is a continual process that we go through. 2 Corinthians 4:16 tells us, "For which cause we faint not; but though our outward man perish, yet the inward man is renewed day by day."

We introduced this thought back in Chapter 6 when we looked at the put on put off process in Ephesians chapter four. This is the put on part of the process. Much of what we have seen until now has been the put off process; that is the messiest part and often the hardest part. Once the old is torn out and cleaned up, the new begins to go in. While we may consider much of our old nature to be unconscious behavior, things that we didn't realize were triggering responses until we stopped and analyzed them, the truth is that at one point it was deliberate choice. We purposely thought about doing the wrong that eventually controlled our lives. It just happened so subtly and distantly that we have forgotten the process took place. Renewing or retraining begins as a conscious process; it begins when we set a stimulus and response in place, and then practice it over and over again until it becomes the normal way of responding without even thinking about it.

This is what Paul had done in his life; that is why he wrote about it so prolifically in so many books of the Bible. In Romans Paul details the transition from the old man to the new from the perspective of the power of sin being cast off. He says in Romans 6:6-14, "Knowing this, that our old man is crucified with him, that the body of sin might be destroyed, that henceforth we should not serve sin. For he that is dead is freed from sin. Now if we be dead with Christ, we believe that we shall also live with him: Knowing that Christ being raised from the dead dieth no more; death hath no more dominion over him. For in that he died, he died unto sin once: but in that he liveth, he liveth unto God. Likewise reckon ye also yourselves to be dead indeed unto sin, but alive unto God through Jesus Christ our Lord. Let not sin therefore reign in your mortal body, that ye should obey it in the lusts thereof. Neither yield ye your members as instruments of unrighteousness unto sin: but yield yourselves unto God, as those that are alive from the dead, and your members as instruments of righteousness unto God. For sin shall not have dominion over you: for ye are not under the law, but under grace."

As a believer, we are not any longer under the power that sin had to hold us bound; but we now have the power through the Holy Spirit of God to put off that old nature and determine to yield our bodies to God. We are alive and can consciously choose righteousness over sinfulness. We must reckon ourselves to be dead to sin and alive to God. The word *reckon* is an accounting term that means "to assign to an account." We are removed from the old account of sin and moved over to the new account of grace, but we must begin to live according to that truth in our daily choices. Paul pointed out that the transaction has been made judicially; it is a matter of the actions catching up to the truth of our standing. Remember what he said in 2 Corinthians 5:17: "Therefore if any man be in Christ, he is a new creature: old things are passed away; behold, all things are become new." Notice the tense of the verse – *is* a new creature, *are* passed away, *are* become new! This is all done if you are saved. Judicially you are made holy, you are righteous before God – now it is time to tear out the old rubbish of the deeds of the old man and replace them with the new man actions that God created you to exhibit. So Paul details that transaction in Ephesians 4:22-32: "That ye put off concerning the former conversation the old man, which is corrupt according to the deceitful lusts; And be renewed in the spirit of your mind; And that ye put on the new man, which after God is created in righteousness and true holiness. Wherefore putting away lying, speak every man truth with his neighbour: for we are members one of another. Be ye angry, and sin not: let not the sun go down upon your wrath: Neither give place to the devil. Let him that stole steal no more: but rather let him labour, working with his hands the thing which is good, that he may have to give to him that needeth. Let no corrupt communication proceed out of your mouth, but that which is good to the use of edifying, that it may minister grace unto the hearers. And grieve not the holy Spirit of God, whereby ye are sealed unto the day of redemption. Let all bitterness, and wrath, and anger, and clamour, and evil speaking, be put away from you, with all malice: And be ye kind one to another, tenderhearted, forgiving one another, even as God for Christ's sake hath forgiven you."

And then again in Colossians 3:1-10: "If ye then be risen with Christ, seek those things which are above, where Christ sitteth on the right hand of God. Set your affection on things above, not on things on the earth. For ye are dead, and your life is hid with Christ in God. When Christ, who is our life, shall appear, then shall ye also appear with him in glory. Mortify therefore your members which are upon the earth; fornication, uncleanness, inordinate affection, evil concupiscence, and covetousness, which is idolatry: For which things' sake the wrath of God cometh on the children of disobedience: In the which ye also walked some time, when ye lived in them. But now ye also put off all these; anger, wrath, malice, blasphemy, filthy communication out of your mouth. Lie not one to another, seeing that ye have put off the old man with his deeds; And have put on the new man, which is renewed in knowledge after the image of him that created him."

Did you notice in these two passages the long list of things that we are to put on in place of the old nature? Look at the list here: labor, giving, edifying speech, kindness, tenderheartedness, forgiveness. All of these things are replacements for the old works that filled up our lives when the flesh was in control. Finding the spiritual opposite and diligently practicing it, renewing our minds, renovating them to resort to the new actions when prompted by the triggers (circumstances that we encounter) is the goal that Paul is trying to get across here.

Paul says it again in Romans 13:12-14: "The night is far spent, the day is at hand: let us therefore cast off the works of darkness, and let us put on the armour of light. Let us walk honestly, as in the day; not in rioting and drunkenness, not in chambering and wantonness, not in strife and envying. But put ye on the Lord Jesus Christ, and make not provision for the flesh, to fulfil the lusts thereof." We are to put on the Lord Jesus Christ in the place of the old man's deeds. The things that Christ would do, we are to do; the way that He would respond is how we are to respond. He is our image to model life after. We are to be conformed to Him. So often we are foolishly holding on to the old image and refusing to yield ourselves to His complete control. The reason that we struggle to accomplish the defeat of the flesh is that we are trying to do it in our own power. The truth is that the Spirit is the only thing that can defeat the flesh; that means that our strong desire to overcome the lusts that the flesh have can only be completely defeated when we fully yield to the Spirit of God in our lives. *Take up your cross*

Remember, the weapons of our warfare are not carnal; you cannot overcome the flesh with the power of the flesh. It must be through yielded obedience to the Spirit, a yielded heart that says, "Lord, what do you want me to put on in place of this old sin?" Then daily by the power of the Spirit of God we must put on Christ and His deeds in place of the old, diligently practicing and establishing them as the natural resort of our hearts until they become second nature to us and we don't have to think about them to do them.

As a young believer, every time I had a trial, I would automatically turn to sinful responses. I got so discouraged, I would beat myself up and weep thinking that I was such a failure as a Christian. I didn't think I could get past the trigger dragging me down; over and over again for years I fell and fell. I felt that life was basically hopeless. As long as things went well, I could live for God; but as soon as there was a trial, my old nature deeds would rise up in my flesh, and I felt powerless again. Little by little, I learned to put off first one thing and then another. They were very small victories at first, but soon they began to be great victories in my life – victory over the dominating spirit of anger, victory over other addictions that had beset me so many times in my life. I remember one of the first things that I grabbed hold of was the thought that the trials were not to drive me to sin; they were to teach me how to live for God. I began to pray earnestly, "Lord, help me learn this lesson so I can grow and not have to fact it again."

It didn't happen overnight. As a matter of fact, the truth is that the more I have learned to put behind me and correct, the more I have seen that I didn't even realize was there; but every victory gave strength for the next. I can honestly say that I know what the victory of the Spirit of God is like in my life, so that the next battle, while still hard, is a joy knowing that each leads me closer to the image of my Saviour which is my life. Every moment and every day, I must depend upon Him and submit to Him, so that the power of the flesh falls away and the power of God rests upon me. What a great joy to be a soldier of the cross and as Paul said in Ephesians 6:11, "Put on the whole armour of God, that ye may be able to stand against the wiles of the devil."

I pray that these things will be a help to you in your journey into the image of Christ in your life, and that you will endure as a good soldier to see the victory that God has in store for you. I promise you that there is nothing like the wonderful presence of God that comes when you have put down the flesh that once dominated you, and you find that the fulfillment of the fruit of the Spirit of God in your life is enough to meet the need.

Renewing of the mind is great and replacing lies with truth is great but "the law of sin" is still stronger than the "law of the mind."